Second Workshop on Extra-Propositional Aspects of Meaning in Computational Semantics

(ExProM 2015)

Held at NAACL HLT 2015

Denver, Colorado, USA
5 June 2015

ISBN: 978-1-5108-0435-7

Printed from e-media with permission by:

Curran Associates, Inc.
57 Morehouse Lane
Red Hook, NY 12571

Some format issues inherent in the e-media version may also appear in this print version.

Printed by Curran Associates, Inc. (2015)

For permission requests, please contact the Association for Computational Linguistics at the address below.

Association for Computational Linguistics
209 N. Eighth Street
Stroudsburg, Pennsylvania 18360

Phone: 1-570-476-8006
Fax: 1-570-476-0860

acl@aclweb.org

Additional copies of this publication are available from:

Curran Associates, Inc.
57 Morehouse Lane
Red Hook, NY 12571 USA
Phone: 845-758-0400
Fax: 845-758-2634
Email: curran@proceedings.com
Web: www.proceedings.com

Introduction

During the last decade, semantic representation of text has focused on extracting propositional meaning, i.e., capturing who does what to whom, when and where. Several corpora are available, and existing tools extract this kind of knowledge, e.g., semantic role labelers trained on PropBank, NomBank or FrameNet. But propositional semantic representations disregard significant meaning encoded in human language. For example, while sentences (1-2) below share the same propositional meaning regarding verb carry, they do not convey the same overall meaning. In order to truly capture what these sentences mean, extra-propositional aspects of meaning (ExProM) such as uncertainty, negation and attribution must be taken into account.

1. Thomas Eric Duncan likely contracted the disease when he carried a pregnant woman sick with Ebola.
2. Thomas Eric personally told me that he never carried a pregnant woman with Ebola.

The Extra-Propositional Aspects of Meaning (ExProM) in Computational Linguistics Workshop focuses on a broad range of semantic phenomena beyond propositional meaning, i.e., beyond linking propositions and their semantic arguments with relations such as AGENT (who), THEME (what), LOCATION (where) and TIME (when).

ExProM is pervasive in human language and, while studied from a theoretical perspective, computational models are scarce. Humans use language to describe events that do not correlate with a real situation in the world. They express desires, intentions and plans, and also discuss events that did not happen or are unlikely to happen. Events are often described hypothetically, and speculation can be used to explain why something is a certain way without a strong commitment. Humans do not always (want to) tell the (whole) truth: they may use deception to hide lies. Devices such as irony and sarcasm are employed to play with words so that what is said is not what is meant. Finally, humans not only describe their personal views or experiences, but also attribute statements to others. These phenomena are not exclusive of opinionated texts. They are ubiquitous in language, including scientific works and news as exemplified below:

- A better team might have prevented this infection.
- Some speculate that this was a failure of the internal communications systems.
- Infected people typically don't become contagious until they develop symptoms.
- Medical personnel can be infected if they don't use protective gear, such as surgical masks and gloves.
- You cannot get it from another person until they start showing symptoms of the disease, like fever.
- You can only catch Ebola from coming into direct contact with the bodily fluids of someone who has the disease and is showing symptoms.

- We've never seen a human virus change the way it is transmitted.
- There is no reason to believe that Ebola virus is any different from any of the viruses that infect humans and have not changed the way that they are spread.

In its 2015 edition, the Extra-Propositional Aspects of Meaning (ExProM) in Computational Linguistics Workshop was collocated with the Conference of the North American Chapter of the Association for Computational Linguistics (NAACL) in Denver, CO. The workshop took place on June 5, 2015, and the program consisted of five papers (4 long papers and 1 short paper) and an invited talk by Lauri Karttunen. ExProM 2015 is a a follow-up of two previous events: the 2010 Negation and Speculation in Natural Language Processing Workshop (NeSp-NLP 2010) and ExProM 2012.

We would like to thank the authors of papers for their interesting contributions, the members of the program committee for their insightful reviews, and Lauri Karttunen for giving the invited talk. We are grateful to the National Science Foundation for a grant to support student travel to the workshop.

Organizers:

Eduardo Blanco, University of North Texas, USA
Roser Morante, VU University Amsterdam, The Netherlands
Caroline Sporleder, Universität Trier, Germany

Program Committee:

Tim Baldwin - The University of Melbourne
Emily M. Bender - University of Washington
Cosmin Adrian Bejan - Vanderbilt University
Gosse Bouma - University of Groningen
Tommaso Caselli - VU University Amsterdam
Jacob Eisenstein - Georgia Tech
Edward Grefenstette - Google DeepMind
Zhou Guadong - Soochow University
Ivan Habernal - TU Darmstadt
Iris Hendrickx - Radboud University
Lori Levin - Carnegie Mellon University
Maria Liakata - University of Warwick
Erwin Marsi - Norwegian University of Science and Technology
Malvina Nissim - University of Groningen
Sampo Pyysalo - University of Turku
Christopher Potts - Stanford University
German Rigau - UPV/EHU
Ellen Riloff - University of Utah
Paolo Rosso - Universidad Politècnica de Valencia
Josef Ruppenhofer - Universität Hildesheim
Roser Saurí - Universitat Pompeu Fabra
Erik Velldal - University of Oslo
Bonnie Webber - University of Edinburgh
Byron C. Wallace, UT Austin
Michael Wiegand - Saarland University

Invited Speaker:

Lauri Karttunen, Stanford University

Table of Contents

Workshop Program

Friday June 5 2015

8:00–09:00 *Breakfast*

9:15–9:30 *Opening remarks*

9:30–10:30 *Invited Talk: Lauri Karttunen*

10:30–11:00 Coffee break

11:00–12:30 Session 1

12:30–2:00 Lunch break

Friday June 5 2015 (continued)

14:00–14:30 Session 2

14:10–14:30 *Committed Belief Tagging on the Factbank and LU Corpora: A Comparative Study*
Gregory Werner, Vinodkumar Prabhakaran, Mona Diab and Owen Rambow

14:30–15:00 *Extending NegEx with Kernel Methods for Negation Detection in Clinical Text*
Chaitanya Shivade, Marie-Catherine de Marneffe, Eric Fosler-Lussier and Albert M. Lai

15:00–15:30 ***Discussion and closing remarks***

Translating Negation: A Manual Error Analysis

Federico Fancellu and Bonnie Webber
School of Informatics
University of Edinburgh
11 Crichton Street, Edinburgh
f.fancellu[at]sms.ed.ac.uk, bonnie[at]inf.ed.ac.uk

Abstract

Statistical Machine Translation has come a long way improving the translation quality of a range of different linguistic phenomena. With negation however, techniques proposed and implemented for improving translation performance on negation have simply followed from the developers' beliefs about why performance is worse. These beliefs, however, have never been validated by an error analysis of the translation output. In contrast, the current paper shows that an informative empirical error analysis can be formulated in terms of (1) the set of semantic elements involved in the meaning of negation, and (2) a small set of string-based operations that can characterise errors in the translation of those elements. Results on a Chinese-to-English translation task confirm the robustness of our analysis cross-linguistically and the basic assumptions can inform an automated investigation into the causes of translation errors. Conclusions drawn from this analysis should guide future work on improving the translation of negative sentences.

1 Introduction

In recent years, there has been increasing interest in improving the quality of SMT systems over a wide range of linguistic phenomena, including coreference resolution (Hardmeier et al., 2014) and modality (Baker et al., 2012). Amongst these, however, translating negation is still a problem that has not been researched thoroughly.

This paper takes an empirical approach towards understanding why negation is a problem in SMT. More specifically, we try to answer two main questions:

1. *What kind* of errors are involved in translating negation?
2. What are the causes of these errors during decoding?

While previous work (section 2) has shown that translating negation is a problem, it has not addressed either of these questions.

The present paper focuses on the first one; we show that tailoring to a semantic task, string-based error categories standardly used to evaluate the quality of the machine translation output, allows us to cover the wide range of errors occurring while translating negative sentences (section 3). We report the results of the analysis of a Hierarchical Phrase Based Model (Chiang, 2007) on a Chinese-to-English translation task (section 4), where we show that all error categories occur to some extent with scope reordering being the most frequent (section 5).

Addressing question (2) requires connecting the assumptions behind this manual error analysis to errors occurring along the translation pipeline. As such, we complete the analysis by briefly introduce an automatic method to investigate the causes of the errors at decoding time (section 6).

Conclusion and future works are reported in section 7 and 8.

Proceedings of the Second Workshop on Extra-Propositional Aspects of Meaning in Computational Semantics (ExProM 2015), pages 1–11,
Denver, Colorado, June 5, 2015.

2 Previous Work

In recent years, automatic recognition of negation has been the focus of considerable work. Following Blanco and Moldoval (2011) and Morante and Blanco (2012) detecting negation is a task of unraveling its structure, i.e. locating in a text its four main components:

- **Cue**: the word or multi-word unit inherently expressing negation (e.g. 'He is not driving a car')
- **Event**: the lexical element the cue directly refers to (e.g. 'He is not driving a car')
- **Scope**: all the elements whose falsity would prove negation to be false; given that the cue is not included, the scope is often discontinuous (e.g. 'He is not driving a car')
- **Focus**: the portion of the statement negation primarily refers to (e.g. 'He is not driving a car).

The *SEM 2012 shared task represented a first attempt to apply machine learning methods to the problem of automatically detect the aforementioned elements in English. In particular CRFs and SVMs, making use of syntactic (both constituent and dependency based) clues, were shown to lead to the best results in a supervised machine learning setting (Read et al., 2012; Chowdhury and Mahbub, 2012). The shared task also saw the release of a fully annotated corpus in the literature domain, which represents, along with the BioScope corpus (Szarvas et al., 2008), the only resource specifically annotated for negation.

There were also a few attempts in automatically detecting negation in Chinese texts. Li et al. (2008) designed a negation detection algorithm based on syntactic patterns; similarly, Zheng et al. (2014) implemented an FSA for automatic recognition of negation structures in Chinese medical texts, using a list of manually defined cues and the syntactic structures they appear in.

In a bilingual setting such as the SMT, however, most work has only considered negation as a side problem. For this reason, no actual analysis on the type of errors involved in translating negation or their causes has been specifically carried out. The standard approach has been to formulate an hypothesis about what can go wrong when translating negation, modify the SMT system in a way aimed at reducing the number of times that happens, and then assume that any increase in BLEU score - the standard automatic evaluation metric used in SMT - confirms the initial hypothesis. Collins et al. (2005) and Li et al. (2009) consider negation, along with other linguistic phenomena, as a problem of *structural mismatch* between source and target; Wetzel and Bond (2012) consider it instead as a problem of *training data sparsity*; finally Baker et al. (2012) and Fancellu and Webber (2014) consider it as a *model problem*, where the system needs enhancement with respect to the semantics of negation. Given that all these works assess the quality of translation of negative sentences using an *n-gram* overlap metric, there is no certainty whether any improvement derives from a better rendering of negation or from other, non-negation related elements.

Evaluating the semantic adequacy of the SMT output has also stimulated interest in recent years. Traditional error categories, such as the ones presented in (Vilar et al., 2006), are mostly based on n-gram overlap between hypothesis and reference and so are the most widely used automatic evaluation metrics used in SMT (e.g. BLEU (Papineni et al., 2002) and TER (Snover et al., 2009)). In contrast, MEANT (Lo and Wu, 2010, 2011) and its human counterpart, HMEANT, attempt to abstract from simple string matching and assess the degree of semantic similarity between machine output and reference sentence. To do so, both sides are annotated using Propbank-like semantic labels, and the fillers matched if both sides contain the same event. To assign a score to the test set evaluated, an F_1 measure over precision and recall of matched fillers is then computed.

3 Methodology

3.1 Manual Annotation

First, we start with the assumption that negation is a language independent semantic phenomenon which can be defined as a structure. This assumption implies that it should be possible to annotate any language using the elements in this structure – **cue**,

event and **scope**. Isolating a small set of semantic elements involved in the construction of negation is useful in the context of SMT to reduce negation into tangible elements at the string level. Moreover each of the three elements above represents different translation problems: if, for instance, translating the *cue* mainly involves ensuring the presence of a negation marker, translating the *scope* involves instead ensuring that semantic elements are translated in the right domain and most of the times, around the negated *event*.

We carried out the annotation of *cue*, *event* and *scope* on both the source Chinese sentences and the correspondent translation output by the SMT system, following the guidelines released during the SEM* 2012 shared task (Morante et al., 2011). To our understanding, this is the first work that applies these guidelines to a language other than English. It is however worth noticing that while these guidelines were released with the goal in mind of automatically extracting information from text, with a particular emphasis on factuality, the present work focuses on translation, where each negation instance is taken into consideration as potential source of error. This leads to some differences in the annotation process, especially in the case of the *event*:

1. While the original guidelines do not annotate negation scoping on non-factual events, such as in conditional clauses (*'if he doesn't come*, I will blame you'), the demands of translation require it to be annotated.

2. While the original guidelines do not include modals or auxiliaries in the event annotation (in order to minimise the number of annotated elements), getting these elements correct in translation is needed to distinguish a correct vs. partially correct event (cf. section 3.2).

3. For the same reason as (2), the event in a nominal predicate includes all its modifiers.

4. All these points apply to Chinese as well; in addition, in the case of resultative constructions (e.g. *fù bù qǐ* lit. 'pay not lift-RES.', 'could not pay, can not afford') we considered the resultative particle as part of the *event*.

With respect to scope, the current work makes a simple approximation: scope is often discontinuous, with multiple semantic units whose translations might impact the overall translation of the scope differently. To facilitate error analysis we approximate the scope in terms of its constituent semantic fillers, here taken to be Propbank-like semantic arguments. In doing so, we consider the scope as the *semantic domain* of negation, where the constituent elements are expected to remain in its boundaries and to preserve their semantic role (or take an equivalent one) during translation.

Example (1) illustrates our annotation scheme over the first instance of *bù* (not) in a Chinese source sentence.

(1) [*wǒmen*]$_{filler}$ *bù*$_{cue}$ *páichú*$_{event}$ [*qízhōng*
We not exclude amidst
yǒu dǎn xīn de huì lái zhǔdòng
there is worried of can come voluntarily
jiāodài]$_{filler}$, *dàn páo de qǐ* bù *gēng*
confess , but run RES not even
duōme?
more Q

Ref: [We]$_{filler}$ do not$_{cue}$ [rule out]$_{event}$ [the possibility that some timid ones might come out and voluntarily confess]$_{filler}$, but would n't many more just run away?

As shown in (1) the scope around the first main clause can be split into two arguments - a subject and an object - around the verb *páichú*(rule out) so error analysis can be carried on each individually. We instead consider the second instance of *bù/not* as 'non-functional negation' and do not annotate it since it is just part of the question and does not constitute itself a negation instance.

3.2 Manual Error Analysis

A subsequent task is to define categories that are able to cover potential errors in translating negation. Our analysis aims at applying a small set of string-based operations traditionally used in SMT to the aforementioned elements of negation. We consider three main operations and apply them to each of the three elements of negation for a total of 9 main conditions:

- **Deletion**: one of the three sub-constituents of negation is present in the source Chinese sentence but not in the machine output. This corresponds to the *missing words* category in (Vilar et al., 2006).
- **Insertion**: the negation element is not present in the source sentence but has been inserted in the machine output. This resembles the *extra words* sub-category in the *incorrect words* class.
- **Reordering**: whether the element has been moved outside its scope. Since some semantic elements can also move inside the scope and take a role which they did not have in the original source sentence, we define the former reordering error as *out-of-scope* reordering error and the latter *intra-scope* reordering error. The reordering category represents an adaptation of the original *word order* category.

Since we are not concerned with errors regarding style, punctuation or unknown words, other operations were left aside.

For a better understanding at *when* during the translation process (a.k.a. the *decoding* process) and *why* the error occurs, we also investigated the trace of rules used to build the 1-best machine output. This is particularly useful in the case of deletion: this may occur because a certain Chinese word or sequence of Chinese words (generally referred in SMT as *phrases*) has not been seen during training (so called *out-of-vocabulary items* - OOVs) and the system is therefore unable to translate them.

After the elements of negation have been annotated in both the source sentences and machine outputs, we use the same heuristic as (H)MEANT (Lo and Wu, 2011) to decide whether a translated unit is *correct* or *partially correct*. We also consider *correct* translations that are synonyms of the source negation element since they are taken to convey the same meaning. This also includes those elements that are negated in the source but are rendered in the machine output by means of a lexical element inherently expressing negation (e.g. *fails*) or by paraphrase into positive (e.g. *bù tóng*, lit. 'not similar' → different). We consider *partially correct* translated elements that do not contain errors which impact the overall meaning. In the case of the event, this might be related to tense agreement or wrong modality, whilst in the case of the scope it is usually related to the fact that secondary elements are not translated correctly but the overall meaning is still preserved.

As in HMEANT, we compute precision, recall and F_1 measure using the following formulae where $e \in E = \{\text{cue,event,filler}\}$. However, unlike HMEANT, we do not normalise the number of correct fillers by the number of total fillers in the predicate.

$$P = \frac{(\sum e_{correct} + 0.5 * \sum e_{partial})}{\sum e_{hyp}}$$

$$R = \frac{(\sum e_{correct} + 0.5 * \sum e_{partial})}{\sum e_{src}}$$

$$F_1 = 2 * \frac{P * R}{P + R}$$

4 System

We carried out the error analysis on the output of the Chinese-to-English hierarchical phrase based system submitted by the University of Edinburgh for the NIST12 MT evaluation campaign.

Hierarchical phrase-based (or HPB) systems are a class of SMT systems that use syntax-like rules and hierarchical tree structures to build an hypothesis translation given a test source sentence and a model previously trained on a bilingual corpora. Unlike pure syntax models, HPBMs do not make use of syntactic constituent tags for non-terminals but instead use an X as placeholder for recursion. A rule used in a Hierarchical Phrase based system looks like the following,

ne veux plus X_1 → do not want X_1 anymore

where the French source (also referred to as the *left hand side* - LHS of the rule) and the English target side (the *right hand side* - RHS) allows arbitrary insertion of another rule where the placeholder X is located.

The system was trained on approximately 2.1 million length-filtered segments in the news domain, with 44678806 tokens on the source and 50452704 on the target, with MGIZA++ (Gao and Vogel,

2008) used for alignment. The system was tuned using MERT (Minimal Error Rate Training, (Och, 2003)) on the NIST06 set.

Two different test sets were considered to assess differences that might be associated with genre: the NIST MT08 test set, containing data from the newswire domain and the IWSLT14 tst2012 test set, containing transcriptions of TED talks. We hypothesise that the difference in genre can influence the kinds of negation related error occurring during translation: as a collection of planned spoken inspirational talks, we expect the IWSLT'14 test set to contain shorter sentences, and on average, more instances of negation. On the contrary, we expect the NIST MT08, where data are from the written language domain, to contain longer sentences and fewer instances of negation.

In order to carry out future work on the effect of word segmentation on the elements on negation, we built two different systems (and therefore *rule tables*), one from data segmented using the LDC-WordSegmenter and the other using the Stanford Word Segmenter. The former matches the segmentation of the NIST08 test set, whilst the latter the one of the IWSLT14 test set.

Out of the 1397 segments in the IWSLT2014 set and the 1357 segments in the NIST MT08 set, 250 sentences for each set were randomly chosen to carry out the manual evaluation.

5 Results

5.1 Manual Analysis

5.1.1 NIST MT08

The results of the manual evaluation for the NIST MT08 test set are reported in Table 1. It can be easily seen that getting the cue right is easier than translating event and scope correctly. The cue is in fact usually a one-word unit and related errors concern almost entirely whether the system has deleted it during translation or not. Event and scope instead are usually multi-word units whose correctness also depends on whether they interact correctly with the other negation elements.

In those cases where the cues were deleted during translation, the trace shows that they were all caused by a rule application that does *not* contain negation on the English right hand side. Also worth noticing is that, in these cases, the negation cue in the source side is lexically linked to the event (*'**bù**shǎo'* , 'not few, many') or lexically embedded in it (e.g. *'dé **bù**dao*, 'cannot obtain'). No cases of cues being deleted were found where the cue is a distinct unit. Also, no cases of cues were found of cues being deleted because of not being seen during training (*out-of-vocabulary items*).

Other cue-related errors involve the cue being reordered with respect to scope. In one case, cue reordering happens within the same scope, where the cue is moved from the main clause to the subordinate. In three other cases, the cue is instead translated outside its source scope and attached to a different event. The two cases are exemplified in (2) and (3) respectively.

(2) [*tā*]$_{filler}$ *cóngbù*$_{cue}$ [*yīnwèi wǒ gěi tā*
She never because I to him
tí guò yìjìan]$_{filler}$ *ér* [*dùi wǒ*]$_{filler}$
raise ASP opinion so to I
huài yǒu$_{event}$ [*pìanjìan*]$_{filler}$ [...]
have bias

Ref: He never showed any bias against me [because i 'd complained to him]$_{sub}$ [...]

Hyp: he **never** mentioned to him because my opinions and i have bias against china [...]

(3) [...] *jiù huì rènwéi bù cúnzài*
[...] then can think not exist

Ref: [...] people would think [that [they do]$_{scope}$ not [exist]$_{scope}$]$_{sub}$

Hyp: [...] do **not** think [there is a]$_{sub}$

As for the translation of events, a trend similar to the translation of cues can be observed, although the percentage of deletions is higher than the cue. The trace shows that in 3 out of 11 cases, deletion is caused by an OOV item, i.e. a Chinese phrase which is not seen in training and for which the system has not learned any translation. The remaining cases resemble the cue case, insofar as no rule contains the target side event. Another problem arising with events is that some fillers in the source might have erroneously become events in the machine output and vice versa; we found 3 events on the source becoming fillers in the target and 7 fillers on the source becoming events in the machine output, as shown in (4).

(4) *zhè yīge jiēduàn de biǎxiàn shì* [*duǎnqī*
This one stage of show is short-term
xiāoguō]$_{filler}$ *bùdà*$_{cue+event}$ [...]
result not big [...]

Ref: what this stage brings forward is : modest success in the short-term [...]

Hyp: this is a stage performance are not$_{cue}$ [short-term effect]$_{event}$

The fact that most of reordering errors are filler-related is connected to the lack of semantic-related information during the translation process, a common problem in machine translation systems. Since there is no explicit guidance as to which events the fillers should be attached to and in what order, *in-scope* and *out-of-scope* problems are to be expected.

Around 10% of filler-related errors were caused by deletion. An investigation of the trace shows that in all 9 cases, the system has knowledge of the source words in the rule table but has applied a rule that does not contain the filler on the target side.

Finally, in the case of fillers, we notice that 2 of the incorrect fillers in the hypothesis were due to the *insertion* in the scope of fillers not present in the source side. The trace shows that this kind of error is generated by rules that contain on the right hand side extra material not related to the source side. We hypothesised that these rules might have been created during training where English words that did not correspond to any Chinese source words were arbitrarily added to neighbouring phrases. For instance, in (5) a rule that translates *yǐzhìyú* ('to the extent of') into 'to the extent of *they*' is used, adding a filler to following negation scope.

(5) [...] *yǐzhìyú wúfǎ yú oū zhou*
[...] to the extent not possible with Europe
méngguó zhèngcháng zhǎnkāi hézuò
union normally open cooperation

Ref: [...] even made it is impossible to carry out cooperation with their European allies as normal .

Hyp: [...] to the extent that [they]$_{filler}$ are unable to conduct normal with its european allies cooperation

NIST MT08 test set					
Average Sentence Length	28				
Number of negated sentences	54		21.6%		
Cue per sentence ratio			1.22%		
	Src		Hyp		
Cues	66		57		
Events	66		57		
Fillers	98		80		
	#	R%	#	P%	F_1
Correct cues	58/66	87.87	53/57	92.98	90.35
Correct events	34/66	51.51	29/57	50.88	
+ Partial events	34 + **8**/66	57.6	29 + **8**/57	57.9	57.74
Correct fillers	48/98	48.97	45/80	56.25	
+ Partial fillers	48 + **9**/98	58.16	45 + **9**/80	67.5	62.48
Deleted cues	4/66	6			
Deleted events	11/66	16.6			
Deleted fillers	9/98	9.18			
Inserted fillers			2/80	2.5	
Reordered cues *same scope*	1/66	1.5	1/57	1.75	
Reordered cues *out of scope*	3/66	4.5			
Reordered events *same scope*	3/66	4.5	7/57	12.2	
Reordered events *out of scope*	1/66	1.5			
Reordered fillers *same scope*	8/98	8.16	5/80	6.25	
Reordered fillers *out of scope*	21/98	21.41			

Table 1: Results from the error analysis of the 250 sentences randomly extracted from the NIST MT08 test set.

5.1.2 IWSLT '14 Tst2012 TED Talks

Results for the TED talks test set are reported in Table 2. It can be observed that results on all three categories are better than the NIST08 test set, in particular for the F_1 measure of correct events and scope. A reduction in the percentage of reordered fillers on the overall number translation errors might be connected to the fact that on average sentences in the TED talk, also given their domain, are shorter than the sentences in the NIST08 test set and therefore there is less chance of operating long range reordering.

We can also observe that genre has an effect on the number of negation cues; despite sentences being shorter, we found more negative instances in the TED talks.

As for the errors in the NIST08 test set, we analysed the trace output after the completion of the translation process to see whether deletions were caused by incorrect rule application or by the presence of OOV items not seen during training. Out of 7 cases of cue deletion, 3 of event deletion and 5 of filler deletion, only one was caused by the presence of an OOV vocabulary item in the source. However, as shown in (6), the OOV error is generated by a wrong segmentation of two elements in the source, *bùzhī* and *zěnme*, which end up being collapsed in a single word unit.

(6) <u>*bùzhīzěnme*</u> *yòng wǒmen bù néng*
do not know how use we not be able
wánquán lǐjiě de fāngshi [...]
completely understand of method [...]

Ref: ways we cannot fully understand that <u>we don't know how to use</u> [...]

Hyp: was converted to the way we cannot fully understand [..]

This seem to exclude OOV items as a problem in translating negation for the present system and what we are left with is a problem of negative elements not correctly reproduced on the target side of the rules.

Finally, we have found two cases of insertion, one cue and the other event related. Overall, cases of insertion are rare and do not constitute a real problem for the system here considered. In general, as for *event* and *scope*, a rule application that does not contain one of these two elements on the Chinese left hand side but inserts it in the English right hand side might be just fortuitous. As in the case of (5), it might have been that a rule containing extra material was preferred because a better fit in that specific context (a LM score is in fact part of the scoring function of a SMT system). Insertion of the *cue* deserves instead a better investigation. The results shows that deletion is sometimes associated with rules whose Chinese (left-hand) side contains a cue whilst the English side does not. This is most certainly caused by the training process where rules are extracted according to what portion of the source Chinese sentence is aligned to what portion in the target English sentence. If an Chinese sentence contains negation but the English does not, a rule learnt from that pair might learn that a negation cue corresponds to something positive. This should theoretically happen the other way around and if so, the application of these rules should lead to insertion. Further analysis of the rule table and the sentences used in training might clarify this point.

6 Towards An Automatic Error Analysis

This manual error analysis assesses the quality of the 1-best translation output by the system. More can be done: (i) we can determine which component of the system is responsible for each error so as to know where to intervene and (ii) we can automate

IWSLT14 tst2012 TED talks					
Average Sentence Length	18				
Number of negated sentences	61		24.4%		
Cue per sentence ratio			1.13%		
	Src		Hyp		
Cues	69		54		
Events	69		52		
Fillers	103		83		
	#	R%	#	P%	F_1
Correct cues	61/69	88.4	53/54	98	92.95
Correct events	48/69	69.56	40/52	76.92	
+ Partial events	48 + **3**/69	71.73	40 + **3**/52	79.8	75.55
Correct fillers	64/103	62	64/83	77	
+ Partial fillers	64 + **3**/103	63.59	64 + **3** /83	78.9	70.42
Deleted cues	7/69	10.14			
Deleted events	5/69	7.2			
Deleted fillers	4/103	3.8			
Inserted cue			1/54	1.8	
Inserted fillers			1/83	1.2	
Reordered events *same scope*	5/69	7.2	1/52	1.9	
Reordered events *out of scope*	4/69	5.7			
Reordered fillers *same scope*	2/103	1.9	6/83	7.2	
Reordered fillers *out of scope*	13/103	12.62			

Table 2: Results from the error analysis of the 250 sentences randomly extracted from the IWSLT2014 test set.

the whole process of error finding. Both actions can be referred to as *automatic error analysis*, given that they rely on (semi-)automatic method to analyse errors in translating negation, although they differ in the scope of their analysis: (i) represents an extension of the manual error analysis, whilst (ii) aims at automating it.

Although out of the scope of the present work, we briefly sketch our current work on (i) whilst leaving (ii) for future work. The reason for this is because the assumption behind this as many other manual analysis, i.e. that a small set of string-based error categories can be used to characterise different kind of translation errors (here semantic), can be easily projected in the automatic error analysis. Moreover, the importance and indispensability of a manual error analysis is highlighted when devising an automatic error analysis. This is obvious in the case of (i), where, in order to find the causes of the errors, we need to know what these are. However, even we succeed in (ii) and we are able to spot errors automatically, we still need a manual error analysis as a benchmark to assess the quality of any automatic method.

When we talk about detecting errors during decoding, we try to determine the reason why our system is behaving differently to what we expect. These expectations depends on the source side negation element processed at each step during decoding and are closely linked to both the set of string-based error category and the set of negation sub-constituents used in this manual error analysis:

1. The **cue** has to be translated correctly; no cue **deletion** or **insertion** should occur.

2. The **event** has to be translated correctly; no event **deletion** or **insertion** should occur.

3. The **cue** has to be connected to right **event**; no cue or event **reordering** should occur.

4. The **semantic arguments** in the source scope should be translated and reproduced in line with the target language semantics; no **deletion**, **insertion** or **reordering** of the semantic fillers should occur.

An ideal system would meet all the above conditions in translating negation in each cell of the decoding chart[1]; if not, we have to inspect the decoding chart trace and classify the errors occurred. The goal here is to find which part of the translation system is responsible for each error category. There are three main type of errors, each one connected to one component of the translation pipeline:

- **Induction errors**, where the correct translation for a given element is absent from the search space. These errors depends on how many target translations are fetched from the rule table when a given source span is translated (default is 20). The more we consider, the more likely is for the correct translation to be inserted in the search space. The system component related to this category is the **rule table**.

- **Search errors**, where the correct translation fetched from the rule table disappears from the search space before making it to the final cell, due to pruning or other optimisation heuristics. The system component responsible for this error is the **search space**.

- **Model errors**, where the system ranks bad translations better than better translations. The component responsible is the **scoring function**.

[1]Hierarchical phrase-based decoder uses a variant of bottom-up CKY chart algorithm

Induction errors occur when no negation element is found in any hypothesis built in any of the chart cell; search errors occur when, by enlarging the search space, hypotheses meeting the expected conditions that were previously absent from the chart are now present; finally, model errors occur where hypothesis meeting one or more expectation are present but rank lower than the ones that do not.

Since these expectations are based on source side elements we need a way to project source side negation elements into a target language; for expectation (1) and (2), we are experimenting with two different methods: (i) via an automatically extracted list of potential cues and a bilingual dictionary enriched with paraphrases; (ii) by extracting cues and events from the multiple reference translations set. To ensure that expectation (3) and (4) are met we instead use a dependency parse.

Preliminary results on the translation of the cue alone (expectation (1)) in the NIST08 MT test set shows that it is uniquely a problem of model error, where good hypotheses are ranked lower than bad ones. A comparison between the scores of good and bad hypotheses show, when the former are not ranked properly, shows that it is the translation model the main responsible for such bad ranking.

7 Conclusion

The present paper presents an analysis of the errors involved in translating negation. We showed that it is possible to build a clear and robust error analysis using (1) the set of semantic elements involved in the meaning of negation (**cue**, **event** and **scope**) and (2) a sub-set of string-based operations traditionally used in SMT error analysis (**deletion**, **insertion** and **reordering**).

Results of a manual error analysis on a Chinese-to-English output shows that this analysis is easily portable to a language other than English and allows us to cover a wide range of potential errors occurring during translating. Our findings also show that amongst the three elements of negation here considered, the *scope* is the most problematic and reordering is in general the most frequent error in Chinese-to-English translation. In the case of deletion or insertion of negation elements, we also found that the errors are attributable to a rule application that prefers positive translations over negative and are therefore not caused by OOV items not seen during training.

Using the assumptions and the results of the manual error analysis, we also introduced an automatic way to inspect the causes of the errors in the decoding chart trace. Preliminary results show that the scoring function is the main responsible for cue deletion errors observed.

We hope that the methodology and the results of the present work can guide future work on improving the translation of negative sentences.

8 Future Work

In the present paper, we have successfully applied the manual error analysis to the output of a Chinese-to-English Hierarchical Phrase-based system. Future work will extend this method to other language pairs and different SMT systems. We in fact expect these two variables to impact the kind of errors found in translation. Chinese and English are in fact very similar in the way they express negation: adverbial negation is the most frequent way of expressing negation (Blanco and Moldoval, 2011; Fancellu and Webber, 2012); morphological negation (or *affixal*) or lexically embedded negation is present in both languages and affect mainly adjectives; events can be both nominal, verbal and adjectival. If we however extend this analysis to a language pair where negation is expressed through different means (e.g. English and Czech), it is unlikely we will find the same error distribution. Moreover, hierarchical phrase-based models are in fact non-purely syntax driven methods that are able to deal with high levels of reordering. That however also means that (a) there is no concept of syntactic constituent boundaries and (b) when reordering is performed incorrectly there is a high degree of element scrambling. For this reason phrase-based systems (where reordering is limited) and syntax-based systems (where an explicit knowledge of constituent boundaries is present) are likely to yield different results.

Finally, this paper has only discussed manual detection of translation errors involving negation. Other ongoing work tries instead to automate this process.

9 Acknowledgements

This work was supported by the GRAM+ grant. The authors would like to thank Adam Lopez for his comments and suggestions and the three anonymous reviewers for their feedback.

References

Baker, Kathryn and Bloodgood, Michael and Dorr, Bonnie J and Callison-Burch, Chris and Filardo, Nathaniel W and Piatko, Christine and Levin, Lori and Miller, Scott (2012). Modality and negation in SIMT use of modality and negation in semantically-informed syntactic MT. *Computational Linguistics*, 38(2):411–438.

Blanco, Eduardo and Moldoval, Dan (2011). Some Issues on Detecting Negation from Text. In *Proceedings of the 24th Florida Artificial Intelligence Research Society Conference (FLAIRS-24)*, pages 228–233, Palm Beach, FL, USA.

Chiang, David (2007). Hierarchical phrase-based translation. *Computational Linguistics*, 33(2):201–228.

Chowdhury, Md and Mahbub, Faisal (2012). FBK: Exploiting phrasal and contextual clues for negation scope detection. In *Proceedings of the First Joint Conference on Lexical and Computational Semantics-Volume 1: Proceedings of the main conference and the shared task, and Volume 2: Proceedings of the Sixth International Workshop on Semantic Evaluation*, pages 340–346.

Collins, Michael and Koehn, Philipp and Kučerová, Ivona (2005). Clause restructuring for statistical machine translation. In *Proceedings of the 43rd Annual Meeting on Association for Computational Linguistics*, pages 531–540.

Fancellu, Federico and Webber, Bonnie (2012). Improving the performance of chinese-to-english Hierarchical phrase-based models (HPBM) on negative data using n-best list re-ranking. Master's thesis, School of Informatics, University of Edinburgh.

Fancellu, Federico and Webber, Bonnie (2014). Applying the semantics of negation to SMT through n-best list re-ranking. *EACL 2014*, page 598.

Gao, Qin and Vogel, Stephan (2008). Parallel implementations of word alignment tool. In *Software Engineering, Testing, and Quality Assurance for Natural Language Processing*, pages 49–57.

Hao-Min, Li and Li, Ying and Duan, Hui-Long and Lv, Xu-Dong (2008). Term extraction and negation detection method in chinese clinical document. *Chinese Journal of Biomedical Engineering*, 27(5).

Hardmeier, Christian and Tiedemann, Jörg and Nivre, Joakim (2014). Translating pronouns with latent anaphora resolution. In *NIPS 2014 Workshop on Modern Machine Learning and Natural Language Processing*.

Li, Jin-Ji and Kim, Jungi and Kim, Dong-Il and Lee, Jong-Hyeok (2009). Chinese syntactic reordering for adequate generation of Korean verbal phrases in Chinese-to-Korean SMT. In *Proceedings of the Fourth Workshop on Statistical Machine Translation*, pages 190–196.

Lo, Chi-kiu and Wu, Dekai (2010). Evaluating machine translation utility via semantic role labels. In *Seventh International Conference on Language Resources and Evaluation (LREC-2010)*, pages 2873–2877.

Lo, Chi-kiu and Wu, Dekai (2011). MEANT: an inexpensive, high-accuracy, semi-automatic metric for evaluating translation utility via semantic frames. In *Proceedings of the 49th Annual Meeting of the Association for Computational Linguistics: Human Language Technologies-Volume 1*, pages 220–229.

Morante, Roser and Blanco, Eduardo (2012). *SEM 2012 shared task: Resolving the scope and focus of negation. In *Proceedings of the First Joint Conference on Lexical and Computational Semantics-Volume 1: Proceedings of the main conference and the shared task, and Volume 2: Proceedings of the Sixth International Workshop on Semantic Evaluation*, pages 265–274.

Morante, Roser and Schrauwen, Sarah and Daelemans, Walter (2011). Annotation of negation cues and their scope, Guidelines v1.0. *Computational linguistics and psycholinguistics technical report series, CTRS-003*.

Och, Franz Josef (2003). Minimum error rate training in Statistical Machine Translation. In *Proceedings of the 41st Annual Meeting on Association for Computational Linguistics-Volume 1*, pages 160–167.

Papineni, Kishore and Roukos, Salim and Ward, Todd and Zhu, Wei-Jing (2002). BLEU: a method for automatic evaluation of machine translation. In *Proceedings of the 40th annual meeting on association for computational linguistics*, pages 311–318.

Read, Jonathon and Velldal, Erik and Øvrelid, Lilja and Oepen, Stephan (2012). Uio 1: constituent-based discriminative ranking for negation resolution. In *Proceedings of the First Joint Conference on Lexical and Computational Semantics-Volume 1: Proceedings of the main conference and the shared task, and Volume 2: Proceedings of the Sixth International Workshop on Semantic Evaluation*, pages 310–318.

Snover, Matthew G and Madnani, Nitin and Dorr, Bonnie and Schwartz, Richard (2009). TER-Plus: paraphrase, semantic, and alignment enhancements to Translation Edit Rate. *Machine Translation*, 23(2-3):117–127.

Szarvas, György and Vincze, Veronika and Farkas, Richárd and Csirik, János (2008). The bioscope corpus: annotation for negation, uncertainty and their scope in biomedical texts. In *Proceedings of the Workshop on Current Trends in Biomedical Natural Language Processing*, pages 38–45.

Vilar, David and Xu, Jia and Haro, Luis Fernando and Ney, Hermann (2006). Error analysis of statistical machine translation output. In *Proceedings of LREC*, pages 697–702.

Wetzel, Dominikus and Bond, Francis (2012). Enriching parallel corpora for statistical machine translation with semantic negation rephrasing. In *Proceedings of the Sixth Workshop on Syntax, Semantics and Structure in Statistical Translation*, pages 20–29.

Zheng Jia and Haomin Li and Meizhi Ju and Yinsheng Zhang and Zhenzhen Huang and Caixia Ge and Huilong Duan (2014). A finite-state automata based negation detection algorithm for chinese clinical documents. In *Progress in Informatics and Computing (PIC), 2014 International Conference on*, pages 128–132.

Filled pauses in User-generated Content are Words with Extra-propositional Meaning

Ines Rehbein
SFB 632 "Information Structure"
Potsdam University
irehbein@uni-potsdam.de

Abstract

In this paper, we present a corpus study investigating the use of the fillers *äh* (uh) and *ähm* (uhm) in informal spoken German youth language and in written text from social media. Our study shows that filled pauses occur in both corpora as markers of hesitations, corrections, repetitions and unfinished sentences, and that the form as well as the type of the fillers are distributed similarly in both registers. We present an analysis of fillers in written microblogs, illustrating that *äh* and *ähm* are used intentionally and can add a subtext to the message that is understandable to both author and reader. We thus argue that filled pauses in user-generated content from social media are words with extra-propositional meaning.

1 Introduction

In spoken communication, we can find a high number of utterences that are disfluent, i.e. that include hesitations, repairs, repetitions etc. Shriberg (1994) estimates the ratio of disfluent sentences in spontaneous human-human communication to be in the range of 5-6%.

One particular type of disfluencies are filled pauses (FP) like *äh* (uh) and *ähm* (uhm). FP are a frequent phenomenon in human communication and can have multiple functions. They can be put at any position in an utterance and are used when a speaker encounters planning and word-finding problems (Maclay and Osgood, 1959; Arnold et al., 2003; Goffman, 1981; Levelt, 1983; Clark, 1996; Barr, 2001; Clark and Fox Tree, 2002), or as strategic devices, e.g. as floor-holders or turn-taking signals (Maclay and Osgood, 1959; Rochester, 1973; Beattie, 1983). Filled pauses can function as discourse-structuring devices, but they can also express extra-propositional aspects of meaning beyond the propositional content of the utterance, e.g. as markers of uncertainty or politeness (Fischer, 2000; Barr, 2001; Arnold et al., 2003).

Examples (1)-(6) illustrate the use of FP to mark repetitions (1), repairs (2), breaks (3) and hesitations (4) (the last one often used to bridge word finding problems). FPs can also express astonishment (5), excitement or negative sentiment (6). Extralinguistic reasons also come into play, such as the lack of concentration due to fatigue or distraction, which might lead to a higher ratio of FP in the discourse.

(1) I will *uh* I will come tomorrow.
(2) I will leave on Sat *uh* on Sunday.
(3) I think I *uh* have you seen my wallet?
(4) I have met Sarah and Peter and *uhm* Lara.
(5) Sarah is Michael's sister. *Uh*? Really?
(6) A: He cheated on her. B: *Ugh*! That's bad!

The role of fillers in spoken language has been discussed in the literature (for an overview, see Corley and Stewart (2008)). Despite this, work on processing disfluencies in NLP has mostly considered them as mere performance phenomena and focused on disfluency detection to improve automatic processing (Charniak and Johnson, 2001; Johnson and Charniak, 2004; Qian and Liu, 2013; Rasooli and

Proceedings of the Second Workshop on Extra-Propositional Aspects of Meaning in Computational Semantics (ExProM 2015), pages 12–21,
Denver, Colorado, June 5, 2015.

Tetreault, 2013; Rasooli and Tetreault, 2014). Far fewer studies have focused on the information that disfluencies contribute to the overall meaning of the utterance. An exception are Womack et al. (2012) who consider disfluencies as extra-propositional indicators of cognitive processing.

In this paper, we take a similar stand and present a study that investigates the use of filled pauses in informal spoken German youth language and in written, but conceptually oral text from social media, namely Twitter microblogs.[1] We compare the use of FP in computer-mediated communication (CMC) to that in spoken language, and present quantitative and qualitative results from a corpus study showing similarities as well as differences between FP in both the spoken and written register. Based on our findings, we argue that filled pauses in CMC are words with extra-propositional meaning.

The paper is structured as follows. Section 2 gives an overview on the different properties of spoken language and written microblogs. In section 3 we present the data used in our study and describe the annotation scheme. Section 4 reports our quantitative results which we discuss in section 5. We complement our results with a qualitative analysis in section 6, and conclude in section 7.

2 Filled Pauses in Spoken and Written Registers

Clark and Fox Tree (2002) propose that FP are *words with meaning*, but so far there is no conclusive evidence to prove this. While experimental results have shown that disfluencies do affect the comprehension process (Brennan and Schober, 2001; Arnold et al., 2003), this is no proof that listeners have access to the *meaning* of a FP during language comprehension but could also mean that FP are produced "unintentionally [...], but at predictable junctures, and listeners are sensitive to these accidental patterns of occurrence." (Corley and Stewart, 2008), p.12.

To show that fillers are words in a linguistic sense, i.e. lexical units that have a specific semantics that is understandable to both speaker and hearer, one would have to show that speakers are able to produce them intentionally and that recipients are able to interpret the intended meaning of a filler.

Assuming that fillers are not linguistic words but simply noise in the signal, caused by the high demands on cognitive processing in spoken online communication, we would not expect to find them in medially written communication such as user-generated content from social media, where the production setting does not put the same time pressure on the user as there is in oral face-to-face communication. However, a search for fillers on Twitter[2] easily proves this wrong, yielding many examples for the use of FP in medially written text (7).

(7) Oh **uh**.. I got into the evolve beta.. yet I have no idea what this game is.. **uhm**..

Both, informal spoken dialogues and microblogs can be described as *conceptually oral*, meaning that both display a high degree of interactivity, signalled by the use of backchannel signals and question tags, and are highly informal with grammatical features that deviate from the ones in the written standard variety (e.g. violations of word order constraints, case marking, etc.). Both registers show a high degree of expressivity, e.g. interjections and exclamatives, and make use of extra-linguistic features (spoken language: gestures, mimics, voice modulation; microtext: emoticons, hashtags, use of uppercased words for emphasis, and more).

Differences between the two registers concern the spatio-temporal setting of the interaction. While spoken language is synchronous and takes place in a face-to-face setting, microblogging usually involves a spatial distance between users and is typically asynchronous, but also allows users to have a *quasi-synchronous* conversation.[3] Quasi-synchronous here means that it is possible to communicate in real time where both (or all) communicating partners are online at the same time, tweeting and re-tweeting in quick succession, but without the need for turn-taking devices as there is a strict first-come-first-serve order for the transmission of the dialogue turns. As a result, microblogging does not put the same time pressure on the user but permits them to monitor and edit the text. This should rule out the use of FP as markers of disfluencies such

[1] See the model of medial and conceptual orality and literacy by Koch & Oesterreicher (1985).

[2] `https://twitter.com/search-home`

[3] See (Dürscheid, 2003; Jucker and Dürscheid, 2012) for an account of *quasi-synchronicity* in online chatrooms.

as repairs, repetitions or word finding problems, and also the use of FP as strategic devices to negotiate who takes the next turn. Accordingly, we would not expect to observe any fillers in written microblogs if their only functions were the ones specified above.

However, regardless of the limited space for tweets,[4] microbloggers make use FP in microtext. This suggests that FP do indeed serve an important communicative function, with a semantics that must be accessible to both the blogger and the recipient.

3 Annotation Experiment

This section describes the data and setup used in our annotation experiment.

3.1 Data

The data we use in our study comes from two different sources. For spoken language, we use the KiezDeutsch-Korpus (KiDKo) (Wiese et al., 2012), a corpus of self-recordings of every-day conversations between adolescents from urban areas. All informants are native speakers of German. The corpus contains spontaneous, highly informal peer group dialogues of adolescents from multiethnic Berlin-Kreuzberg (around 266,000 tokens excluding punctuation) and a supplementary corpus with adolescent speakers from monoethnic Berlin-Hellersdorf (around 111,000 tokens). On the normalisation layer where punctuation is included, the token counts add up to around 359,000 tokens (main corpus) and 149,000 tokens (supplementary corpus).

The first release of KiDKo (Rehbein et al., 2014) includes the transcriptions (aligned with the audio files), a normalisation layer, and a layer with part-of-speech (POS) annotations as well as non-verbal descriptions and the translation of Turkish code-switching.

The data was transcribed using an adapted version of the transcription inventory GAT 2 (Selting et al., 1998), also called GAT minimal transcript, which uses uppercased letters to encode the primary accent and hyphens in round brackets to mark silent pauses of varying length.

The microblogging data consists of German-language Twitter messages from different regions

[4]The maximum length of a tweet is limited to 140 characters.

	KiDKo		Twitter	
äh	646	35.8	6403	0.6
ähm	360	19.9	4182	0.4
both	1,006	55.7	10,585	1.0
# tokens	180,558	10,000	105,074,399	10,000

Table 1: Distribution of *äh* and *ähm* in KiDKo and Twitter microtext (raw counts (grey column) and normalised numbers (white column) per 10,000 tokens).

of Germany, and includes 7,311,960 tweets with 105,074,399 tokens. For retrieving the tweets we used the Twitter Search API[5] which allows one to specify the user's location by giving a latitude and a longitude pair as parameters for the search. Over a time period of 6 months we collected tweets from 48 different locations.[6] The corpus was automatically augmented with a tokenisation layer and POS tags.[7]

A string search in both corpora, looking for variants of *äh* and *ähm* (including upper- and lowercased spelling variants with multiple *ä*, with and without a *h*, and with one or more *m*) shows the following distribution (Table 1). Filled pauses are far less frequent in microblogs compared to spoken language, but due to the large amount of data we can easily extract more than 10,000 instances from the Twitter corpus. Note that the tweets in our corpus come from different registers like news, ads, public announcements, sports, and more, with only a small portion of private communication. When constraining the corpus search to the subsample of private tweets, we will most likely find a higher proportion of FP in the social media data.

In summary, we observe a higher amount of FP in spoken language than in Twitter microblogs. However, in both corpora variants of *äh* outnumber *ähm* by roughly the same factor. This observation is compatible with the results of (Womack et al., 2012) who report that around 60% of the FP in their corpus of English diagnostic medical narratives are nasal filled pauses (*uhm, hm*) and around 40% are non-nasal (*uh, er, ah*).

[5]https://dev.twitter.com/docs/api

[6]Note that the Twitter geoposition parameter can only approximate the regional origin of the speakers as the location where a tweet has been sent is not necessarily the residence or place of birth of the tweet author.

[7]Unfortunately, for legal reasons we are not allowed to distribute the data.

	Categories	Position
1	Repetition	**B/I**
2	Repair	**B/I**
3	Break	**B/I**
4	Hesitation	**B/I**
5	Question	**B/I**
6	Interjection	**B/I**
7	Unknown	

Table 2: Labels used for annotating the fillers (B: between utterances; I: integrated in the utterance).

	Twitter		KiDKo	
Sample	*äh*	*ähm*	*äh*	*ähm*
1	n.a.	n.a.	0.79	0.75
2	n.a.	0.84	0.73	0.64
3	0.80	0.83	0.78	0.84
4	0.87	0.87	0.78	0.75
5	0.86	0.86	0.74	n.a.
avg. κ	**0.84**	**0.85**	**0.76**	**0.75**

Table 3: Inter-annotator agreement (κ) for 3 annotators.

3.2 Annotating Fillers in Spoken Language and in Microtext

To be able to compare the use of fillers in spoken language with the one in Twitter microtext, we extract samples from the two corpora including 500 utterances/tweets with at least one use of *äh* and 500 tweets with at least one instance of *ähm*. At the time of the investigation, the transcription of KiDKo was not yet completed, and we only found 360 utterances including an *ähm* in the finished transcripts.

For annotation, we used the BRAT rapid annotation tool (Stenetorp et al., 2012). Our annotation scheme is shown in Table 2. We distinguish between different categories of fillers, namely between FP that mark repetitions, repairs, hesitations, or that occur at the end of an unfinished utterance/tweet (breaks). We also annotated variants of *äh* and *ähm* which were used as question tags or interjections, but do not consider them as part of the disfluency markers we are interested in. The Unknown label was used for instances which either do not belong to the filler class and shouldn't have been extracted, such as example (8), or which couldn't be disambiguated, usually due to missing context.

(8) Hääähähh !!!

Each filler is labelled with its *category* and *position*. By *position* we mean the position of the filler in the utterance or tweet. Here we distinguish between fillers which occur between (B) utterances/at the beginning or end of tweets (example 9b) and those which are integrated (I) in the utterance/tweet (9a). The numbers in the first column of Table 2 correspond to examples (1)-(6).

(9) a. das 's irgend so 'n **äh** (-) RAPper der ...
this 's some such a **uh** rapper who ...

this is some **uh** rapper who ... (Hesitation-I)

b. **äh** weiß ich nich
uh know I not

uh I don't know (Hesitation-B)

3.3 Inter-Annotator Agreement

The data was divided into subsamples of 100 utterances/tweets. Each sample was annotated by three annotators. Table 3 shows the inter-annotator agreement (Fleiss' κ) on the KiDKo and Twitter samples. We report agreement for all but three samples which we used to train the annotators, refine the guidelines and to discuss problems with the annotaton scheme. As we had only 360 instances of *ähm* from KiDKo, we divided them into three samples with 100 utterances and a fourth sample with 60 utterances.

Table 3 shows that the annotation of fillers is not an easy task. The disagreements in the annotations concern both the category and the position of the FP. In some cases the annotators agree on the label but disagree on the position of the filler (10a). This can be explained by the fact that spoken language (and sometimes also tweets) does not come with sentence boundaries, and it is often not clear where we should segment the utterance. In example (10a) two annotators interpreted the reparandum as part of the utterance and thus assigned REPAIR-I, while the third annotator analysed *am Samstag* (on Saturday) as a new utterance, resulting in the label REPAIR-B.

(10) a. SPK39 trifft sich am SONNtag mit
SPK39 meets REFL on-the Sunday with
den SPK23 **ÄH** am SAMStag
the SPK23 uh on-the Saturday
"SPK39 meets SPK23 on Sunday uh on Saturday"

b. wir HAM dann **ÄH** wir ham halbe stunde
we have then uh we have half hour
UNterricht
class
"then we have uh we have class for half an hour"

More often, however, the disagreements concern the category of the filler, as in (10b) where two annotators analysed the utterance as a repair while the third annotator interpreted it as a break followed by a new start. The results show that the annotation of fillers in KiDKo seems to be much harder, with average κ scores around 0.1 lower than for the tweets.

4 Quantitative Results

Table 4 shows that the ranking for the different categories of *äh* and *ähm* is the same in both corpora (11). Hesitations are the most frequent category marked by *äh* and *ähm*, followed by repairs and breaks. Repetitions are less frequent, especially in the written microblogs, as are *äh* and *ähm* as question tags and interjections.

(11) Hesitation > Repairs > Breaks > Repetitions > Questions/Interjections

äh/ähm	KiDKo		Twitter	
	#	%	#	%
Hesitations	557	64.78	759	72.91
Repairs	105	12.21	191	18.35
Breaks	88	10.23	52	0.05
Repetitions	53	6.16	9	0.01
Questions	10	1.16	6	0.01
Interjections	11	1.28	5	0.00
total	860=100%		1041=100%	

Table 4: Frequencies of *äh/ähm* in KiDKo and in Twitter (note: numbers don't add up to 100% because of *Unknown* cases).

However, we can also observe a substantial difference between the spoken and the written register. In the latter one, the two most frequent categories, hesitations and repairs, make up for more than 90% of all instances of *äh* and *ähm*, while in spoken language these two categories only account for 76-77% of all occurrences of the two fillers. A possible explanation is that breaks and repetitions in spoken language are either performance phenomena or caused by discourse strategies (e.g. floor-holding) which are both superfluous in asynchronous written communication. This still leaves us with the question why hesitations and repairs do occur in written text at all. We will come back to this question in section 6.

The next question we ask is whether the two forms, *äh* and *ähm*, are used interchangeably or whether the use of each form is correlated with its function. As shown in Table 5, hesitations and breaks are more often marked by *ähm* while *äh* occurs more frequently as a marker of repairs and repetitions. This observation holds for both the spoken and the written register. 72.8% and 80.0% of all instances of *ähm* occur in the context of a hesitation in KiDKo and Twitter, while only 59.0% (KiDKo) and 65.8% (Twitter) of the non-nasal fillers *äh* are used to mark a hesitation. A Fisher's exact test shows that for hesitations and repairs, the differences are statistically significant with $p < 0.01$ and $p < 0.05$, while for breaks and repetitions, the differences might be due to chance.

Next we look at the syntactic position where those fillers occur in the text. We would like to know how often FP are integrated in the utterance and how often they occur between utterances.

	KiDKo %		Twitter %	
	äh	*ähm*	*äh*	*ähm*
Hesitation	59.0	72.8	65.8	80.0
Break	9.0	11.9	4.5	5.5
Repair	16.1	5.8	25.4	11.5
Repetition	7.4	4.2	1.2	0.6

Table 5: Distribution of *äh* and *ähm* between different types of disfluencies.

		KiDKo %		Twitter %	
		B	I	B	I
äh	Hesitations	24.6	34.4	42.6	23.2
	Repairs	0.1	16.0	0.6	24.8
	Repetitions	0.0	7.4	0.2	1.0
ähm	Hesitations	31.4	41.4	62.4	17.6
	Repairs	0.0	5.8	0.4	11.1
	Repetitions	0.0	4.2	0.0	0.6

Table 6: Position of *äh* and *ähm* in correlation to their category.

Fox et al. (2010) present a cross-linguistic study on self-repair in English, German and Hebrew, and observe that self-corrections in English often include the repetition of whole clauses, i.e. English speakers "recycle" back to the subject pronouns (Fox et al. 2010:2491). In their German data this pattern was less frequent. Fox et al. (2010) conclude that morpho-syntactic differences between the languages have an influence on the self-repair practices in the speakers.

Our findings are consistent with Fox et al. (2010) in that we mostly observe the repetition of words, not of clauses (Table 6). Nearly all fillers which mark repetitions are integrated in the utterance or tweet, only a few occur between utterances/tweets. Fillers as markers of repairs are also mostly integrated.

For hesitations, the most frequent category, we get a more diverse picture. In our spoken language data, *äh* and *ähm* are more often integrated in the utterance, while for tweets FP as hesitation markers mostly appear at the beginning or end of the tweet.

So far, our quantitative investigation showed some striking similarities in the use of filled pauses in the two corpora. In both registers, the ranking of the different disfluency types marked by the FP were the same. Furthermore, we showed that speakers/users are sensitive to the surface form of a FP and prefer to use *äh* in repairs and *ähm* in hesitations, regardless of the medium they use for communication.

5 Discussion

In this section we will look at related work on FP and try to put our findings into context. Previous work on the difference between nasal and non-nasal fillers (Barr, 2001; Clark and Fox Tree, 2002) has described nasal fillers such as *uhm, hm* as indicators of a high cognitive load, while their non-nasal variants indicate a lower cognitive load during speech production. Clark and Fox Tree (2002) have proposed the *filler-as-word hypothesis*, stating that FP like *uh* and *uhm* are words in a linguistic sense with the basic meaning that a minor (*uh*) or major (*uhm*) delay in speaking is about to follow. This analysis is based on a corpus study showing that silent pauses following a nasal filler are longer than silent pauses after a non-nasal filler. Beyond the basic meaning, FP can have different implicatures, depending on the context they are used in, such as indicating that the speaker wants to keep the floor, is planning the next (part of the) utterance, or wants to cede the floor. To illustrate this, Clark and Fox Tree (2002) use *goodbye* which has the basic meaning "express farewell" but, when uttered while someone is approaching the speaker, can have the implicature "Go away".

We take the *filler-as-word hypothesis* of Clark and Fox Tree (2002) as our starting point and see how adequate it is to describe the use of FP in written microblogs (section 6). However, we try to avoid the term *implicature* which seems problematic in this context, as we are not dealing with implicatures built on regular lexical meanings but rather with implicatures on top of non-propositional meaning. As a side-effect, the implicatures based on filled pauses are not cancellable.

The analysis of Clark and Fox Tree (2002) is not uncontroversial (see, e.g., Womack et al. (2012) for a short discussion on that matter). O'Connell and Kowal (2005) criticise that the corpus study of Clark and Fox Tree (2002) is based on pause length as perceived by the annotators (instead of being analysed by means of acoustic measurements).

Furthermore, it might be possible that the semantics of FP to indicate the length of a following delay only applies to English. Belz and Klapi (2013) have measured pause lengths after nasal and non-nasal fillers in German L1 and L2 dialogues from a MAP task and could not find a similar correlation between filler type and pause length.

In summary, it is not clear whether the different findings are due to methodological issues, or might be particular to certain languages and text types. Shriberg (1994), p.130 suggests that for English, models of disfluencies based on the ATIS corpus, a corpus of task-oriented dialogues about air travel planning, might not be able to predict the behaviour of disfluencies in spoken language corpora with data recorded in a less restricted setting.

The MAP task corpora used in Belz and Klapi (2013), for example, includes dialogues where one speaker instructs another speaker to reproduce a route on a map. Due to the functional design, the content of the dialogues is constrained to solving the task at hand and thus the language is expected to differ from the one used in the London–Lund corpus (Svartvik, 1990), a corpus of personal communication, that was used by Clark and Fox Tree (2002).

Fox Tree (2001) presents a perception experiment showing that *uh* helps recognizing upcoming words, while the nasal *um* doesn't. In our study we found a strong correlation between the category of the filler and its form (nasal vs. non-nasal). Nasal fillers were mostly used in the context of hesitations, which is consistent with their ascribed basic function as indicators of longer pauses (Clark and Fox Tree, 2002). The tendency to use *äh* within repairs might be explained by Fox Tree (2001)'s findings that non-nasal fillers help to recognise the next word. Thus, we would expect a preference for non-nasal FP to be used as an interregnum before the repair.

Other evidence comes from Brennan and Schober (2001) who present experiments where the subjects had to follow instructions and select objects on a graphical display. They showed that insertions of *uh* after a mid-word interruption in the instruction helped the subjects to correctly identify the target object, as compared to the same instruction where the filler was replaced by a silent pause. They conclude that fillers help to recover from false information in repairs.[8]

So far, our findings are consistent with previous work outlined above, but do not rule out other explanations. A major argument against the analysis of FP as linguistic words is that so far there is no conclusive evidence that speakers do produce them intentionally (Corley and Stewart, 2008).

Our corpus study provides this evidence by showing that FP in CMC are produced deliberately and intentionally. Furthermore, we observed a statistically significant correlation between filler form (nasal or non-nasal) and filler category, which also points at *äh* and *ähm* being separate words with distinguishable meanings.

In the next section, we show that FP in CMC can add a subtext to the original message that can be understood by the recipients, and that the information they add goes beyond the contribution made by nonverbal channels such as facial expressions or gestures. We illustrate this, based on a qualitative analysis of our Twitter data.

6 Extra-propositional Meaning of FP in Social Media Text

New text from social media provides us with a good test case to investigate whether filled pauses are words with (extra-propositional) meaning, as the production of written text is to a far greater extent subject to self-monitoring processes. This means that we can confidently rule out that the use of fillers in tweets is due to performance problems caused by the time pressure of online communication. Another important point is that communication on Twitter is not synchronous but can be time-delayed and works on a first-come-first-serve basis. This is quite important, as it means that we can also exclude the discourse-strategic functions of FP (e.g. floor-holding and turn-taking) as possible explanations for the use of fillers in user-generated microtext.

We conclude that there have to be other explanations for the use of filled pauses as markers of hesitations and repairs in microblogs. Consider the following examples (12)-(14).

(12) Mein ... **ääh** Glückwunsch! RT @germanpsycho: Ich bin nun verheiratet.
My ... **uh** congratulation! RT @germanpsycho: I am now married.
"My ... **uh** congratulations! RT @germanpsycho: I'm married now."

(13) Die hat aber schöne **ähm** Augen.
This one has PTCL beautiful **uhm** eyes.
"This one has really beautiful **uhm** eyes."

(14) Ich frage für, **ähm**, einen Freund.
I ask for, **uhm**, a friend.
"I'm asking for **uhm** a friend."

[8] Unfortunately, they did not compare the effect of *uh* in repairs to the one obtained by a nasal filler like *um*.

The fillers in the examples above add a new layer of meaning to the tweet which results in an interpretation different from the one we get without the filler. While a simple "Congratulations!" as answer to the message "I'm married now" would be interpreted as a polite phrase, the mere addition of the filler implies that this tweet should not be taken at face value and has a subtext along the lines "Actually, I really feel sorry for you". The same is true for (13) where the subtext can be read as "In fact, we're talking about some other bodyparts here". In example (14), the subtext added by the filler will most probably be interpretated as "I'm really asking for myself but won't admit it".[9]

In the next examples (15)-(17), also hesitations, the filler is used to express the author's uncertainty about the proposition.

(15) 30000 € für die 2h db Show für regiotv...
30000 € for the 2h db show for regiotv...
ähm...? Ich weiss grad auch nich..
uhm...? I know just now also not..
"30000 € for the 2h db show for regiotv... **uhm**...? I don't know right now, either.."

(16) Tor für #Arminia durch, **ääh**, wir glauben Schütz.
Goal for #Arminia by **uuh**, we believe Schütz.
"Goal for #Arminia by **uuh**, we believe Schütz."

(17) @zinken **äh**.. so 98%
@zinken **uh**.. around 98%
"@zinken **uh**.. around 98%"

Thus, the most general commonality between the examples above is that the speaker does not make a commitment concerning the truth content of the message.

The following examples (18)-(21) show instances of *äh* and *ähm* in repairs where the FP occur as *interregnum* between *reparandum* and *repair*.[10]

I will leave you $\underbrace{\textit{on Sat}}$ $\underbrace{\textit{uh}}$ $\underbrace{\textit{on Sunday}}$

REPARANDUM INTERREGNUM REPAIR

[9]In fact, this adds an interesting meta-level to the utterance, as by inserting the filler the author draws attention to the fact that there is something she seemingly wants to hide.

[10]We follow the terminology of Shriberg (1994).

The tweet author enacts a slip of the tongue, either by using homonymous or near-homonymous words (Diskus (discus) – Discos (discos), hängst (hang) – Hengst (stallion)) or by using analogies and conventionalised expressions (off – on, resist – contradict). The "mistake" was made with humorous intention and is then corrected. The filler takes again the slot of the interregnum and serves as a marker of the intended pun.

(18) Ob Diskuswerfer früher immer in
Whether discus-throwers in the past always in
Diskus *äh* **Discos** geübt haben, etwa als
discus *uh* **discos** trained have, perhaps as
Rauswerfer am Eingang?
bouncers at the entrance?
"In the past, have discus-throwers always trained in **discus** *uh* **discos**, maybe as bouncers at the entrance?"

(19) Du **Hengst**! *äh*, **hängst**.
You **stallion**! *uh*, **hang**.
"You **stallion**! *uh*, **hang**."

(20) MacBook aus, Handy aus, TV aus. Buch **an**,
MacBook off, mobile off, TV off. Book **on**,
ähh, **aufgeklappt**.
uhh, **open**.
"MacBook off, mobile off, TV off. Book **on**, *uhh*, **open**."

(21) wer könnte Dir schon **widerstehen**, *ähm*, ich
who could you PTCL **resist**, *uhm*, I
meine **widersprechen**.
mean **contradict**.
"who could **resist** you, *uhm*, I mean **contradict**."

In the next set of examples, (22)-(24), a taboo word or word with a strong negative connotation is reformulated into something more socially acceptable (minister of propaganda → district mayor; madness → spirit; tantalise → educate). Often, this is done with a humorous intention, but also to express negative sentiment (e.g. in (22) towards Buschkowsky, or in (23) towards Apple).

(22) Exakt. Wie es das Buch von eurem
Exactly. How it the book of your
RMVP Minister Goebbels *äh*
RMVP minister Goebbels *uh*
Bezirksbürgermeister Buschkowsky so
district mayor Buschkowsky so
beschrieben hat. :-)
described has :-)

"Exactly. Just as the book of your **minister of propaganda Goebbels** *uh* **district mayor Buschkowsky** has described :-)"

(23) Du hast den Apple **Wahnsinn**... *äh*, **Spirit**
You have the Apple **madness**... *uh*, **spirit**
einfach noch nicht verstanden ;)
simply still not understood ;)
"You haven't yet understood the Apple **madness**... *uh* **spirit** ;)"

(24) ... ein bisserl Nachwuchs **quäl**... *ähm*
... a little bit new blood **tant**... *uhm*
ausbilden
educating
"... **tant[alising]** the new blood *uhm* **educating**"

These examples show that the use of *äh* and *ähm* in tweets is intentional and highly edited. The two forms are used to express the speaker's uncertainty about the propositional content of the message, or as a signal that the speaker does not warrant the truth of the message. Other functions include the use of fillers as markers of humorous intentions and of negative sentiment (see Table 7). Note that the meanings are not necessarily distinct but often overlap.

We thus argue that FP in user-generated content from social media are linguistic words that are produced intentionally and have an extra-propositional meaning that can be understood by the recipients.

Meaning	Description
UNCERTAINTY	Speaker is uncertain about the propositional content
TRUTH CONTENT	Speaker does not warrant the truth content of the proposition
HUMOR	Marker of humorous intention
EVALUATION	Marker of negative sentiment

Table 7: Extra-propositional meaning of fillers in CMC.

7 Conclusions

The results from our corpus study show that fillers in user-generated text from social media are linguistic words that are produced intentionally and function as carriers of extra-propositional meaning.

This finding has consequences for work on Sentiment Analysis and Opinion Mining in social media text, as it shows that FP are used as a marker of irony and humour in Twitter, and also indicate uncertainty and negative sentiment. Thus, filled pauses might be useful features for irony detection, sentiment analysis, or to assess the strength of an opinion in online debates.

Acknowledgments

This research was supported by a grant from the German Research Association (DFG) awarded to SFB 632 "Information Structure". I am grateful to Sören Schalowski and Josef Ruppenhofer for valuable comments and discussions that contributed to this work. I would also like to thank our annotators, Nadine Reinhold and Emiel Visser, and the anonymous reviewers for their thoughtful comments.

References

Jennifer E. Arnold, Maria Fagnano, and Michael K. Tanenhaus. 2003. Disfluencies signal theee, um, new information. *Journal of Psycholinguistic Research*, 32(1):25–36.

Dale J. Barr, 2001. *Trouble in mind: paralinguistic indices of effort and uncertainty in communication*, pages 597–600. Paris: L'Harmattan.

Geoff W. Beattie. 1983. *Talk: an analysis of speech and non-verbal behaviour in conversation*. Milton Keynes: Open University Press.

Malte Belz and Myriam Klapi. 2013. Pauses following fillers in L1 and L2 German Map Task dialogues. In *The 6th Workshop on Disfluency in Spontaneous Speech*, DiSS.

Susan E. Brennan and Michael F. Schober. 2001. How listeners compensate for disfluencies in spontaneous speech. *Journal of Memory and Language*, 44:274–296.

Eugene Charniak and Mark Johnson. 2001. Edit detection and parsing for transcribed speech. In *Proceedings of the Second Meeting of the North American Chapter of the Association for Computational Linguistics on Language Technologies*, NAACL.

Herbert H. Clark and Jean E. Fox Tree. 2002. Using uh and um in spontaneous speech. *Cognition*, 84:73–111.

Herbert H. Clark. 1996. *Using language*. Cambridge: Cambridge University Press.

Martin Corley and Oliver W. Stewart. 2008. Hesitation disfluencies in spontaneous speech: The meaning of um. *Language and Linguistics Compass*, 2:589–602.

Christa Dürscheid. 2003. Medienkommunikation im Kontinuum von Mündlichkeit und Schriftlichkeit. Theoretische und empirische Probleme. *Zeitschrift für angewandte Linguistik*, 38:3756.

Kerstin Fischer. 2000. *From cognitive semantics to lexical pragmatics: the functional polysemy of discourse particles*. Mouton de Gruyter: Berlin, New York.

Barbara Fox, Yael Maschler, and Susanne Uhmann. 2010. A cross-linguistic study of self-repair: evidence from English, German and Hebrew. *Journal of Pragmatics*, 42:2487–2505.

Jean E. Fox Tree. 2001. Listeners' uses of um and uh in speech comprehension. *Memory and Cognition*, 2(29):320–326.

Erving Goffman, 1981. *Radio talk*, pages 197–327. Philadelphia, PA: University of Pennsylvania Press.

Mark Johnson and Eugene Charniak. 2004. A tag-based noisy channel model of speech repairs. In *Proceedings of the 42Nd Annual Meeting on Association for Computational Linguistics*, ACL.

Andreas H. Jucker and Christa Dürscheid. 2012. The linguistics of keyboard-to-screen communication. A new terminological framework. *Linguistik Online*, 6(56):39–64.

Peter Koch and Wulf Oesterreicher. 1985. Sprache der Nähe – Sprache der Distanz. Mündlichkeit und Schriftlichkeit im Spannungsfeld von Sprachtheorie und Sprachgeschichte. *Romanistisches Jahrbuch*, 36:15–43.

Willem J.M. Levelt. 1983. Monitoring and self-repair in speech. *Cognition*, 14:41–104.

Howard Maclay and Charles E. Osgood. 1959. Hesitation phenomena in spontaneous English speech. *Word*, 15:19–44.

Daniel C. O'Connell and Sabine Kowal. 2005. Uh and um revisited: Are they interjections for signaling delay? *Journal of Psycholinguistic Research*, 34(6):555–576.

Xian Qian and Yang Liu. 2013. Disfluency detection using multi-step stacked learning. In *Proceedings of the 2013 Conference of the North American Chapter of the Association for Computational Linguistics: Human Language Technologies*, NAACL-HLT.

Sadegh Mohammad Rasooli and Joel Tetreault. 2013. Joint parsing and disfluency detection in linear time. In *Proceedings of the 2013 Conference on Empirical Methods in Natural Language Processing*, EMNLP.

Sadegh Mohammad Rasooli and Joel Tetreault. 2014. Non-monotonic parsing of fluent umm i mean disfluent sentences. In *Proceedings of the 14th Conference of the European Chapter of the Association for Computational Linguistics*, EACL.

Ines Rehbein, Sören Schalowski, and Heike Wiese. 2014. The KiezDeutsch Korpus (KiDKo) release 1.0. In *The 9th International Conference on Language Resources and Evaluation*, LREC.

Sherry R. Rochester. 1973. The significance of pauses in spontaneous speech. *Journal of Psycholinguistic Research*, 2(1):51–81.

Margret Selting, Peter Auer, Birgit Barden, Jörg Bergmann, Elizabeth Couper-Kuhlen, Susanne Günthner, Uta Quasthoff, Christoph Meier, Peter Schlobinski, and Susanne Uhmannet. 1998. Gesprächsanalytisches Transkriptionssystem (GAT). *Linguistische Berichte*, 173:91–122.

Elizabeth Ellen Shriberg. 1994. *Preliminaries to a Theory of Speech Disfluencies*. Ph.D. thesis, University of California at Berkeley.

Pontus Stenetorp, Sampo Pyysalo, Goran Topić, Tomoko Ohta, Sophia Ananiadou, and Jun'ichi Tsujii. 2012. Brat: a Web-based Tool for NLP-Assisted Text Annotation. In *Proceedings of the Demonstrations at the 13th Conference of the European Chapter of the Association for Computational Linguistics*, EACL.

Jan Svartvik. 1990. *The London Corpus of Spoken English: Description and Research*. Lund: Lund University Press.

Heike Wiese, Ulrike Freywald, Sören Schalowski, and Katharina Mayr. 2012. Das KiezDeutsch-Korpus. Spontansprachliche Daten Jugendlicher aus urbanen Wohngebieten. *Deutsche Sprache*, 2(40):797–123.

Kathryn Womack, Wilson McCoy, Cecilia Ovesdotter Alm, Cara Calvelli, Jeff B. Pelz, Pengcheng Shi, and Anne Haake. 2012. Disfluencies as extra-propositional indicators of cognitive processing. In *Proceedings of the Workshop on Extra-Propositional Aspects of Meaning in Computational Linguistics*, ExProM '12.

A Compositional Interpretation of Biomedical Event Factuality

Halil Kilicoglu, Graciela Rosemblat, Michael J. Cairelli, Thomas C. Rindflesch
National Library of Medicine
National Institutes of Health
Bethesda, MD, 20894
{kilicogluh,grosemblat,mike.cairelli,trindflesch}@mail.nih.gov

Abstract

We propose a compositional method to assess the factuality of biomedical events extracted from the literature. The composition procedure relies on the notion of semantic embedding and a fine-grained classification of extra-propositional phenomena, including modality and valence shifting, and a dictionary based on this classification. The event factuality is computed as a product of the extra-propositional operators that have scope over the event. We evaluate our approach on the GENIA event corpus enriched with certainty level and polarity annotations. The results indicate that our approach is effective in identifying the certainty level component of factuality and is less successful in recognizing the other element, negative polarity.

1 Introduction

The scientific literature is rich in extra-propositional phenomena, such as speculations, opinions, and beliefs, due to the fact that the scientific method involves hypothesis generation, experimentation, and reasoning to reach, often tentative, conclusions (Hyland, 1998). Biomedical literature is a case in point: Light et al. (2004) estimate that 11% of sentences in MEDLINE abstracts contain speculations and argue that speculations are more important than established facts for researchers interested in current trends and future directions. Such statements may also have an effect on the reliability of the underlying scientific claim. Despite the prevalence and importance of such statements, natural language processing systems in the biomedical domain have largely focused on more foundational tasks, including named entity recognition (e.g., disorders, drugs) and relation extraction (e.g., biological events, gene-disease associations), the former task addressing the *conceptual* level of meaning and the latter addressing the *propositional* level.

The last decade has seen significant research activity focusing on some extra-propositional aspects of meaning. The main concern of the studies that focused on the biomedical literature has been to distinguish facts from speculative, tentative knowledge (Light et al., 2004). The studies focusing on the clinical domain, on the other hand, have mainly aimed to identify whether findings, diseases, symptoms, or other concepts mentioned in clinical reports are present, absent, or uncertain (Uzuner et al., 2010). Various corpora have been annotated for relevant phenomena, including hedges (Medlock and Briscoe, 2007) and speculation/negation (Vincze et al., 2008; Kim et al., 2008). Several shared task challenges with subtasks focusing on these phenomena have been organized (Kim et al., 2009; Kim et al., 2012). Supervised machine learning and rule-based approaches have been proposed for these tasks. In general, these studies have been presented as extensions to named entity recognition or relation extraction systems, and they often settle for assigning discrete values to propositional meaning elements (e.g., assessing the *certainty* of an *event*).

Kilicoglu (2012) has proposed a unified framework for extra-propositional meaning, encompassing phenomena discussed above as well as discourse level relations, such as Contrast and Elaboration, generally ignored in the studies of extra-propositional meaning (Morante and Sporleder, 2012). The framework uses *semantic embedding* as the core notion, *predication* as the represen-

Proceedings of the Second Workshop on Extra-Propositional Aspects of Meaning in Computational Semantics (ExProM 2015), pages 22–31,
Denver, Colorado, June 5, 2015.

tational means, and *semantic composition* as the methodology. It relies on a fine-grained linguistic characterization of extra-propositional meaning, including modality, valence shifters, and discourse connectives. In the current work, we present a case study of applying this framework to the task of assessing biomedical event *factuality* (whether an event is characterized as a fact, a counter-fact, or merely a possibility), an important step in determining current trends and future directions in scientific research. For evaluation, we rely on the meta-knowledge corpus (Thompson et al., 2011), in which biological events from the GENIA event corpus (Kim et al., 2008) have been annotated with several extra-propositional phenomena, including certainty level, polarity, and source. We discuss in this paper how two of these phenomena relevant to factuality (certainty and polarity) can be inferred from the semantic representations extracted by the framework. Our results demonstrate that certainty levels can be captured correctly to a large extent with our method and indicate that more research is needed for correct polarity assessment.

2 Related Work

Modality and negation are the two linguistic phenomena that are often considered in computational treatments of extra-propositional meaning. Morante and Sporleder (2012) provide a comprehensive overview of these phenomena from both theoretical and computational linguistics perspectives. In the FactBank corpus (Saurí and Pustejovsky, 2009), events from news articles are annotated with their factuality values, which are modeled as the interaction of *epistemic modality* and *polarity* and consist of eight values: FACT, PROBABLE, POSSIBLE, COUNTER-FACT, NOT PROBABLE, NOT CERTAIN, CERTAIN BUT UNKNOWN, and UNKNOWN. Saurí and Pustejovsky (2012) propose a factuality profiler that computes these values in a top-down manner using lexical and syntactic information. They capture the interaction between different factuality markers scoping over the same event. de Marneffe et al. (2012) investigate *veridicality* as the pragmatic component of factuality. Based on an annotation study that uses FactBank and MechanicalTurk subjects, they argue that veridicality judgments should be modeled as probability distributions. They show that context and world knowledge play an important role in assessing veridicality, in addition to lexical and semantic properties of individual markers, and use supervised machine learning to model veridicality. Szarvas et al. (2012) draw from previous categorizations and annotation studies to introduce a unified subcategorization of semantic uncertainty, with EPISTEMIC and HYPOTHETICAL as the top level categories. Re-annotating three corpora with this subcategorization and analyzing type distributions, they show that out-of-domain data can be gainfully exploited in assessing certainty using domain adaptation techniques, despite the domain- and genre-dependent nature of the problem.

In the biomedical domain, several corpora have been annotated for extra-propositional phenomena, in particular, negation and speculation. The GENIA event corpus (Kim et al., 2008) contains biological events from MEDLINE abstracts annotated with their certainty level (CERTAIN, PROBABLE, DOUBTFUL) and assertion status (EXIST, NON-EXIST). The BioScope corpus (Vincze et al., 2008) consists of abstracts and full-text articles as well as clinical text annotated with negation and speculation markers and their scopes. While they clearly address similar linguistic phenomena, the representations used in these corpora are significantly different (cue-scope representation vs. tagged events), and there have been attempts at reconciling these representations (Kilicoglu and Bergler, 2010; Stenetorp et al., 2012). BioNLP shared tasks on event extraction (Kim et al., 2009; Kim et al., 2012) and CoNLL 2010 shared task on hedge detection (Farkas et al., 2010) have focused on GENIA and BioScope negation/speculation annotations, respectively. Supervised machine learning techniques (Morante et al., 2010; Björne et al., 2012) as well as rule-based methods (Kilicoglu and Bergler, 2011) have been attempted in extracting these phenomena and their scopes. Wilbur et al. (2006) propose a more fine-grained annotation scheme with multi-valued qualitative dimensions to characterize scientific sentence fragments: *certainty* (complete uncertainty to complete certainty), *evidence* (from no evidence to explicit evidence), *polarity* (positive or negative), and *trend/direction* (increase/decrease, high/low). In a similar vein, Thompson et al. (2011) annotate each event in the GENIA event corpus with five *meta-knowledge* elements: Knowledge Type (Investigation, Observation, Analysis, Method, Fact, Other), Certainty Level (considerable speculation, some speculation, and certainty), Polarity (negative and positive), Manner (high, low, neutral), and Source (Current, Other). Their annotations are more semantically precise as they are applied to events, rather than somewhat arbitrary sentence fragments used by Wilbur et al. (2006). Miwa et al. (2012) use a machine learning-based approach to assign meta-knowledge categories to events. They cast the task as a classification problem and use syntactic (dependency paths), semantic (event structure), and discourse features (location of the sentence within the abstract). They apply their system to BioNLP shared task data, as well, overall slightly outperforming the state-of-the-art systems.

3 Methods

We provide a brief summary of the framework here, mainly focusing on *predication* representation, embedding predicate categorization, and the compositional algorithm.

3.1 Predications

The framework uses the *predication* construct to represent all levels of relational meaning. A predication consists of a predicate *P* and *n* logical arguments (logical subject, logical object, adjuncts). They can be nested; in other words, they can take other predications as arguments. We call such constructs *embedding predications* to distinguish them from *atomic predications* that can only take atomic terms as arguments. While some embedding predications operate at the basic propositional level, extra-propositional meaning is exclusively captured by embedding predications. We use the notion of *semantic scope* to characterize the structural relationships between predications. A predication Pr_1 is said to *embed* a predication Pr_2 if Pr_2 is an argument of Pr_1. Similarly, a predication Pr_2 is is said to be within the *semantic scope* of a predication Pr_1, if a) Pr_1 embeds Pr_2, or b) there is a predication Pr_3, such that Pr_1 embeds Pr_3 and Pr_2 is within the semantic scope of or shares an argument with Pr_3. Scope relations play an important role in the composition procedure. A predication also encodes the *source* (*S*) and *scalar modality value* of the predication (MV_{Sc}). A formal definition of predication, then, is:

$$Pr := [P, S, MV_{Sc}, Arg_{1..n}], n >= 1$$

By default, the source of a predication is the writer of the text (*WR*). The source may also indicate a term or predication that refers to the source (i.e., who said what is described by the predication? what is the evidence for the predication?). The scalar modality value of the predication is a value in the [0,1] range on a relevant modality scale (*Sc*), which is assigned according to lexical properties of the predicate *P* and modified by its discourse context. By default, an unmarked, declarative statement has the scalar modality value of 1 on the EPISTEMIC scale (denoted as $1_{epistemic}$), corresponding to a fact.

3.2 Categorization

With the embedding categorization, we aim to provide a fine-grained characterization of the kinds of extra-propositional meanings contributed by predicates that indicate embedding. A synthesis of various linguistic typologies and classifications, the categorization is similar to the certainty subcategorization proposed by Szarvas et al. (2012); however, it not only targets certainty-related phenomena, but is rather a more general categorization of embedding predicates that indicate extra-propositional meaning. We distinguish four main classes of embedding predicates: MODAL, RELATIONAL, VALENCE_SHIFTER and PROPOSITIONAL; each class is further divided into subcategories. For the purposes of this paper, MODAL and VALENCE_SHIFTER categories are most relevant (illustrated in Figure 1).

A MODAL predicate associates its embedded predication with a modality value on a scale determined by the semantic category of the modal predicate (e.g., EPISTEMIC scale, DEONTIC scale). The scalar modality value (MV_{Sc}) indicates how strongly the embedded predication is associated with the scale *Sc*, 1 indicating strongest positive association and 0 negative association. VALENCE_SHIFTER predicates do not introduce new scales but trigger a scalar shift of the embedded predication on the associated scale.

The MODAL subcategories relevant for factuality computation and examples of predicates belonging to these categories are as follows:

- EPISTEMIC predicates indicate a judgement about the factual status of the embedded predication (e.g., *may, possible*).

- EVIDENTIAL predicates indicate the type of evidence (observation, inference, etc.) for the embedded predication (e.g., *demonstrate, suggest*).

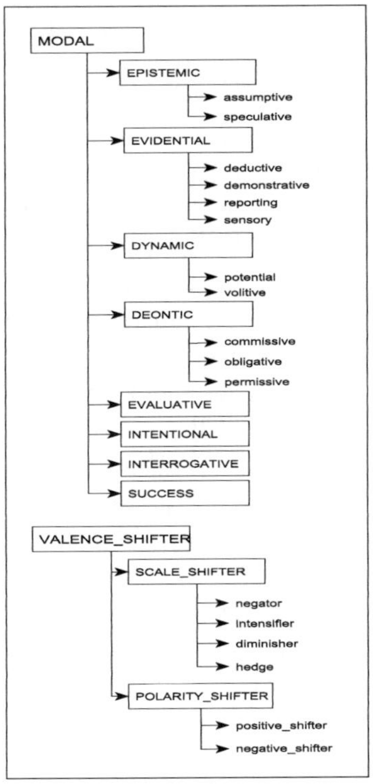

Figure 1. Embedding predicate types.

- DYNAMIC predicates indicate ability or willingness towards an event (e.g., *able, want*).
- INTENTIONAL predicates indicate effort of an agent to perform an event (e.g., *aim*).
- INTERROGATIVE predicates indicate questioning or inquiry towards the embedded event (e.g., *investigate*).
- SUCCESS predicates indicate degree of success associated with the embedded predication (e.g., *manage, fail*).

Each subcategory is associated with its own modality scale, except the EVIDENTIAL category, which is associated with the EPISTEMIC scale. The categories listed above also have secondary epistemic readings, in addition to their primary scale; for example, INTERROGATIVE predicates can indicate uncertainty. The EPISTEMIC scale is the most relevant scale to investigate factuality. Our model of this scale and how modal auxiliaries correspond to it is illustrated in Figure 2. It is similar to the characterization of factuality values by Saurí and Pustejovsky (2012), although numerical epistemic values are assigned to predications ($MV_{epistemic}$), rather than discrete values like Probable or Fact. In this, the characterization follows that of Nirenburg and Raskin (2004), which lends itself more readily to the type of operations proposed for scalar modality values.

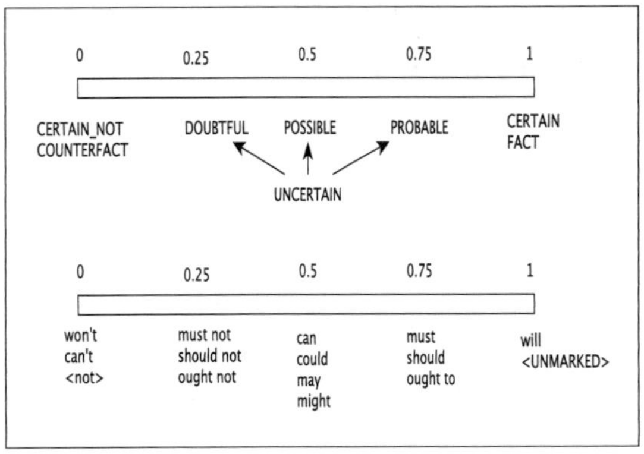

Figure 2. The epistemic scale with characteristic values and corresponding modal auxiliaries.

The SCALE_SHIFTER subcategory of valence shifters also plays a role in factuality assessment. Predicates belonging to this category change the scalar modality value of the predications in their scope. The subtypes of this category are NEGATOR, INTENSIFIER, DIMINISHER, and HEDGE. A DIMINISHER predicate (e.g., *hardly*) lowers the modality value, while an INTENSIFIER increases it (e.g., *strongly*). On the other hand, a negation marker belonging to the NEGATOR category (e.g., *no* in *no indication*) inverts the modality value of the embedded predication. The HEDGE category contains *attribute hedges* (e.g., *mostly, in general*) (Hyland, 1998), whose effect is to make the embedded predication more vague. We model this by decreasing, increasing or leaving unchanged the modality value depending on the position of the embedded predication on the scale.

Lexical and semantic knowledge about predicates belonging to embedding categories are encoded in a dictionary, which currently consists of 987 predicates, 544 of them belonging to MODAL and 95 to SCALE_SHIFTER categories. A very preliminary version of this dictionary was introduced in Kilicoglu and Bergler (2008). It was later extended and refined using several corpora and linguistic classifications (including Saurí (2008) and Nirenburg and Raskin (2004)). Since predicates collected from external resources do not neatly fit into embedding categories and we target deeper levels of meaning distinctions, the dictionary construction involved a fair amount of manual refinement. The dictionary encodes the lemma and part-of-speech of the predicate as well as its extra-propositional meaning senses. Each sense consists of five elements:

1. *Embedding category*, such as ASSUMPTIVE.
2. *Prior scalar modality value* (if any).
3. *Embedding relation classes* indicate the semantic dependencies used to identify the logical object argument of the predicate.
4. *Scope type* indicates whether the predicate allows a wide or narrow scope reading (for example, in *I don't think that P*, because *think* allows narrow scope reading, the negation is transferred to its complement (*I think that not P*)).
5. *Argument inversion* (true/false) determines whether the object and subject arguments should be switched in semantic interpretation.

Lemma	*may*	
POS	*MD* (modal)	
Sense.01	Category	SPECULATIVE
	Scalar modality value	0.5
	Embedding rel. classes	*AUX*
Sense.02	Category	PERMISSIVE
	Scalar modality value	0.6
	Embedding rel. classes	*AUX*

Table 1. Dictionary entry for *may*.

The entry in Table 1 indicates that the modal auxiliary *may* is associated with two modal senses (i.e., it is ambiguous) with differing scalar modality values. It also indicates that a predication embedded by SPECULATIVE *may* will be assigned the epistemic value of 0.5 initially. *Scope type* and *argument inversion* attributes are not explicitly given, indicating default values for each.

3.3 Composition

Semantic composition is the procedure of bottom-up predication construction using the knowledge encoded in the dictionary and syntactic information in the form of dependency relations. Dependency relations are extracted using the Stanford CoreNLP toolkit (Manning et al., 2014). We use the Stanford collapsed dependency format (de Marneffe et al., 2006) for dependency relations. We illustrate the salient steps of this procedure on a sentence from the GENIA event corpus (sentence 9 from PMID 10089566 shown in row (1) in Table 2). For brevity, the simplified version of the sentence is given in row (2), in which textual spans are substituted with the corresponding event annotations.

As the first step in the procedure, the syntactic dependency graphs of sentences of a document are combined and transformed into a semantically enriched, directed, acyclic semantic document graph through a series of dependency transformations. The nodes of the semantic graph correspond to textual units of the document and the direction of the arcs reflects the direction of the *semantic dependency* between its endpoints. The transformation is guided by a set of rules, illustrated on row (3). For example, the first three transformations are due to the Verb Complex Transformation rule, which reorders the dependencies that a verb is involved in such that semantic scope relations with the auxiliaries and other verbal modifiers are made explicit. The resulting semantic dependencies on the right indicate that *involve* is within the scope of *not*, which in turn is in the scope of *may*, and the entire verb complex *may not involve* is within the scope of *thus*, which indicates a discourse relation.

The next steps of the compositional algorithm, *argument identification* and *scalar modality value composition*, play a role in factuality assessment[1]. *Argument identification* is the process of determining the logical arguments of a predication, based on the bottom-up traversal of the semantic graph. It is guided by *argument identification rules*, each of which defines a mapping from a lexical category and an embedding class to a logical argument type. Such a rule applies to a predicate specified in the dictionary that belongs to the lexical category and serves as the head of a semantic dependency labeled with the embedding relation class. With argument identification rules, we determine, for example, that the second instance of *may* in the example, has as its logical object, the predication indicated by *operate*, since there is an *AUX* embedding relation between *may* and *operate*, which satisfies the constraint defined in the embedding dictionary (Table 1).

Scalar modality value composition is the procedure of determining the relevant scale for a predication and its modality value on this scale. The following principles are applied:

1. Initially, every predication is assigned to

[1]The compositional steps that we do not discuss here are *source propagation* and *argument propagation*.

(1)	*Thus HIV-1 gp41-induced IL-10 up-regulation in monocytes may not involve NF-kappaB, MAPK, or PI3-kinase activation, but rather may operate through activation of adenylate cyclase and pertussis-toxin-sensitive Gi/Go protein to effect p70(S6)-kinase activation.*	
(2)	*Thus* E_{27} *may not* E_{32}, E_{33}, *or* E_{34}, *but rather may* E_{39} *and* E_{40}.	
(3)	*advmod(involve,thus)* *aux(involve,may)* *neg(involve,not)* *prep_of(activation,cyclase)*	*ADVMOD(thus,may)* *AUX(may,not)* *NEG(not,involve)* *PREP_OF(activation,adenylate cyclase)*
(4)	*involve*:CORRELATION(E_{32}, *WR*, $0.5_{epistemic}$, E_{27}, E_{28}) *not*:NEGATOR(EM_{53}, *WR*, $0.5_{epistemic}$, E_{32}) *may*:SPECULATIVE(EM_{57}, *WR*, $1.0_{epistemic}$, EM_{53}) *operate*:REGULATION(E_{39}, *WR*, $0.5_{epistemic}$, E_{38}, E_{27}) *may*:SPECULATIVE(EM_{58}, *WR*, $1.0_{epistemic}$, E_{39})	

Table 2. Composition example for 10089566:S9.

EPISTEMIC scale with the value of 1 (i.e., a fact).

2. A MODAL predicate places its logical object on the relevant MODAL scale and assigns to it its prior scalar modality value, specified in the dictionary.

3. A SCALE_SHIFTER predicate does not introduce a new scale but changes the existing scalar modality value of its logical object.

4. The scalar influence of an embedding predicate (*P*) extends beyond the predications it embeds to another predication in its scope (Pr_e), if one of the following constraints is met:

    - *P* is associated with the epistemic scale and the intermediate predications (Pr_i) are either of SCALE_SHIFTER type or are associated with epistemic scale
    - *P* is of SCALE_SHIFTER type and at most one intermediate predication is of MODAL type
    - *P* is of a non-epistemic MODAL type and Pr_i all belong to SCALE_SHIFTER type

Assuming that we have a predicate *P* which indicates an embedding predication *Pr* and a predication (Pr_e) under its scalar influence, the scalar modality value of Pr_e is updated differently, based on whether the predicate *P* is a MODAL or a SCALE_SHIFTER predicate. All update operations used for MODAL predicates are given in Table 3 and those for SCALE_SHIFTER predicates in Table 4. For MODAL predicates, the composition is modeled as the interaction of the prior scalar modality value of the embedding predicate ($MV_{Sc}(P_{modal})$) in the first column and the current scalar modality value associated with the embedded predication ($MV_{Sc}(Pr_e)$) in the second column, resulting in the value shown in the third column ($MV_{Sc}(Pr_e)'$). When *P* is a scale-shifting predicate, the update procedure is guided by its type, as illustrated in Table 4. *X* and *Y* represent arbitrary values in the range of [0,1].

	$MV_{Sc}(P_{modal})$	$MV_{Sc}(Pr_e)$	$MV_{Sc}(Pr_e)'$
(1)	= X	= 1.0	X
(2)	= X	= 0.0	1-X
(3)	> Y	> 0.5 ∧ = Y	min(0.9, Y+0.2)
(4)	< Y ∧ >= 0.5	> 0.5 ∧ = Y	min(0.5,Y-0.2)
(5)	< 0.5	> 0.5 ∧ = Y	1-Y
(6)	>= 0.5	< 0.5 ∧ = Y	Y
(7)	< 0.5	< 0.5 ∧ = Y	1- Y

Table 3. The composition of scalar modality values in MODAL contexts.

For the example shown in Table 2, the computation in row (1) of Table 3 applies when we encounter the SPECULATIVE *may* node dominating the *operate* node in the semantic graph: since $MV_{epistemic}(may)$=0.5 and *operate* at the time of composition has epistemic value of 1, its scalar modality value gets updated to 0.5.

When *not*, a NEGATOR, is encountered in composition, the scalar modality value of its embedded predication (*involve*) is updated to 0, due to row (2) in Table 4 (1-1=0). In the next step of composition, when the first instance of SPECULATIVE *may* is encountered, the nodes in its scope, *not* and

	Type	$MV_{Sc}(Pr_e)$	$MV_{Sc}(Pr_e)'$
(1)	NEGATOR	= 0.0	0.5
(2)	NEGATOR	> 0.0 ∧ = Y	1-Y
(3)	INTENSIFIER	(= 0.0 ∨ = 1.0) ∧ = Y	Y
(4)	INTENSIFIER	>= 0.5 ∧ = Y	min(0.9,Y+0.2)
(5)	INTENSIFIER	< 0.5 ∧ = Y	max(0.1,Y-0.2)
(6)	DIMINISHER	(= 0.0 ∨ = 1.0) ∧ = Y	Y
(7)	DIMINISHER	>= 0.5 ∧ = Y	max(0.5,Y-0.2)
(8)	DIMINISHER	< 0.5 ∧ = Y	max(0.4,Y+0.2)
(9)	HEDGE	= 0.0	0.2
(10)	HEDGE	= 1.0	0.8
(11)	HEDGE	= Y	Y

Table 4. The composition of scalar modality values in SCALE_SHIFTER contexts.

involve, have epistemic values of 1 and 0, respectively. The scalar modality value of *not* gets updated to *min(0.5,1-0.2)=0.5* (row (4) in Table 3). Row (2) in Table 3 applies to *involve*, resulting in 0.5 as its new epistemic value (1-0.5).

Row (4) in Table 2 shows the annotations generated by the system. The system takes as input GENIA event annotations (e.g., CORRELATION and REGULATION), which we expand with scalar modality values and sources. For example, E_{32}..E_{34}, three events triggered by *involve* and annotated as CORRELATION events in GENIA, have epistemic value of 0.5 and WR as the source (only one of the events, E_{32}, is shown for brevity). The system also generates other embedding predications (indicated with *EM*) corresponding to fine-grained extra-propositional meaning. To clarify, the content of first three predications (first an event and the latter two extra-propositional) are expressed in natural language below:

- E_{32}: Correlation between gp41-induced IL-10 upregulation and NF-kappaB activation is POSSIBLE according to the author.
- EM_{53}: That there is no correlation between gp41-induced IL-10 upregulation and NF-kappaB activation is POSSIBLE according to the author.
- EM_{57}: That it is possible there no correlation between gp41-induced IL-10 upregulation and NF-kappaB activation is a FACT according to the author.

3.4 Data and Evaluation

We assessed our methodology on the meta-knowledge corpus (Thompson et al., 2011), in which GENIA events are annotated with certainty levels (CL) and polarity. This corpus consists of 1000 MEDLINE abstracts and contains 34,368 event annotations. Uncertainty is only annotated in this dataset for events with Analysis knowledge type. Such events correspond to 17.6% of the entire corpus. Of all Analysis events, 33.6% are annotated with L2 (high confidence), 11.4% with L1 (low confidence), and 55% with L3 (certain) CL values. Polarity, on the other hand, is annotated for all events (6.1% negative).

Factuality values are often modeled as discrete categories (e.g., PROBABLE, FACT). Thus, to evaluate our approach, we converted the scalar modality values associated with predications (MV_{Sc}) to discrete CL and polarity values using mapping rules, shown in Table 5. The rules were based on the analysis of 100 abstracts that we used for training.

Condition	Annotation
$MV_{epistemic} = 0 \vee MV_{epistemic} = 1$	L3
$MV_{epistemic} > 0.6 \wedge MV_{epistemic} < 1$	L2
$MV_{epistemic} > 0 \wedge MV_{epistemic} <= 0.6$	L1
$MV_{potential} > 0$	L2
$MV_{interrogative} = 1 \vee MV_{intentional} = 1$	L1
$MV_{epistemic} = 0 \vee MV_{potential} = 0 \vee MV_{success} = 0$	Negative

Table 5. Mapping scalar modality values to event certainty and polarity.

We evaluated CL mappings in two ways: a) we restricted it only to Analysis type events, the only ones annotated with L1 and L2 values, and b) we evaluated them on the entire corpus. For polarity, we only considered the entire corpus. As evaluation metrics, we calculated precision, recall, and F_1 score as well as accuracy on the discrete values we obtained by the mapping.

Another evaluation focused more directly on factuality. We represented the gold CL-polarity pairs as numerical values and calculated the average distance between these values and those generated by the system. The lower the distance, the better the system can be considered. In this evaluation scheme, annotating a considerably speculative (L1) event as somewhat speculative (L2) is penalized less than annotating it as certain (L3). We mapped the gold annotations to the numerical values as follows: L3-Positive → 1, L2-Positive → 0.8, L1-Positive → 0.6, L1-Negative → 0.4, L2-Negative → 0.2, L3-Negative → 0.

4 Results and Discussion

The results of mapping the system annotations to discrete values annotated in the meta-knowledge corpus are provided in Table 6.

Type	Precision	Recall	F_1	Accuracy
CL evaluation limited to Analysis events				
CL				81.75
L3	78.43	95.57	86.15	
L2	90.65	61.46	73.25	
L1	83.22	76.28	79.60	
Evaluation on the entire test set				
CL				95.13
L3	97.27	97.74	97.51	
L2	73.08	61.55	66.61	
L1	61.42	76.28	68.05	
Polarity				95.32
Positive	95.99	99.15	97.54	
Negative	74.17	37.04	49.41	

Table 6. Evaluation results.

When the CL evaluation is limited to Analysis events, we obtain an accuracy of approximately 82%. The baseline considered by Miwa et al. (2012) is the majority class, which would yield an accuracy of 55% for these events. Their CL evaluation is not limited to Analysis events, and they report F_1 scores of 97.6%, 66.5%, and 74.9% for L3, L2, and L1 levels, respectively, on the test set. Restricting the system to Analysis events, we obtain the results shown at the top of the table (86.2%, 73.3%, and 79.6%). Lifting the Analysis restriction, we obtain the results shown at the bottom (97.5%, 66.6%, and 68.1% for L3, L2, and L1, respectively). The results are very similar for L3 and L2 levels, while our system somewhat underperformed on L1. With respect to negative polarity, our system performed poorly (49.4% vs. Miwa et al.'s 63.4%), while the difference was minor for positive polarity (97.5% vs. 97.7%).

In comparing to Miwa et al.'s results, several points need to be kept in mind. First, in contrast to their study, we have not performed any training on the corpus data, except determining the mapping rules shown in Table 5. Secondly, knowing whether an event is an Analysis event or not is a significant factor in determining the CL value and their machine learning features are likely to have exploited this fact, whereas we did not attempt to identify the knowledge type of the event. Thirdly, L1 and L2 values appear only for Analysis events, therefore the evaluation scenario that only considers Analysis events is likely to overestimate the performance of our system on L1 and L2 and underestimate it on L3.

While our system performed similarly to Miwa et al.'s with regards to positive polarity, our mappings for negative polarity were less successful, which suggests that modeling negative polarity as the lower end of several modal scales (the last row of Table 5) may not be sufficient for correctly capturing the polarity values. Our preliminary analysis of the results indicate that scope relationships between predications could play a more significant role. In other words, whether an event is in the scope of a predication trigger by a NEGATOR predicate may be a better predictor of negative polarity.

With the evaluation scheme that is based on average distance, we obtained a distance score of 0.12. For the majority class baseline, this score would be 0.21. Our score shows clear improvement over the baseline; however, it is not directly comparable to Miwa et al.'s results. This evaluation scheme, to our knowledge, has not previously been used to evaluate factuality and we believe it is better suited to the gradable nature of factuality.

Analyzing the results, we note that many errors are due to problems in dependency relations and transformations that rely on them. Errors in dependency relations are common due to complexity of the language under consideration, and these errors are further compounded by hand-crafted transformation rules that can at times be inadequate in capturing semantic dependencies correctly. In the following example, the prepositional phrase attachment error caused by syntactic parsing (*to suppress...* is attached to the main verb *result*, instead of to *ability*) prevents the system from identifying the semantic dependendency between *ability* and *suppress*, causing a L2 recall error. While the system uses a transformation rule to correct some prepositional phrase attachment problems, this particular case was missed.

- *The reduction in gene expression resulted from the ability of IL-10 to suppress IFN-induced assembly of signal transducer ...*

- *prep_to(result,suppress)* vs. *prep_to(ability,suppress)*

Prior scalar modality values in the dictionary have been manually determined and are fixed.

They are able to capture the meaning subtleties to a large extent and the composition procedure attempts to capture the meaning changes due to markers in context. However, some uncertainty markers are clearly more ambiguous than others, leading to different certainty level annotations in similar contexts and our method may miss these differences due to the fixed value in the dictionary. For example, the adjective *potential* has been almost equally annotated as an L1 and L2 cue in the meta-knowledge corpus. This also seems to confirm the finding of de Marneffe et al. (2012) that world knowledge and context have an effect on the interpretation of factuality.

We also noted what seem like annotation errors in the corpus. For example, in the sentence *L-1beta stimulation of epithelial cells did not generate any ROIs*, the event expressed with *generation of ROIs* seems to have negative polarity, even though it is not annotated as such in the corpus.

5 Conclusion

We presented a rule-based compositional method for assessing factuality of biological events. The method is linguistically motivated and emphasizes generality over corpus-specific optimizations, and without making much use of the corpus for training, we were able to obtain results that are comparable to the performance of the state-of-the-art systems for certainty level assignments. The method was less successful with respect to polarity assessment, suggesting that the hypothesis that negative polarity can be modeled as corresponding to the lower end of the modal scales may be inadequate. In future work, we plan to develop a more nuanced approach to negative polarity.

Acknowledgments

This work was supported by the intramural research program at the U.S. National Library of Medicine, National Institutes of Health.

References

Jari Björne, Filip Ginter, and Tapio Salakoski. 2012. University of Turku in the BioNLP'11 Shared Task. *BMC Bioinformatics*, 13 Suppl 11:S4.

Marie-Catherine de Marneffe, Bill MacCartney, and Christopher D. Manning. 2006. Generating typed dependency parses from phrase structure parses. In *Proceedings of the 5th International Conference on Language Resources and Evaluation*, pages 449–454.

Marie-Catherine de Marneffe, Christopher D. Manning, and Christopher Potts. 2012. Did it happen? The pragmatic complexity of veridicality assessment. *Computational Linguistics*, 38(2):301–333.

Richárd Farkas, Veronika Vincze, György Móra, János Csirik, and György Szarvas. 2010. The CoNLL-2010 Shared Task: Learning to Detect Hedges and Their Scope in Natural Language Text. In *Proceedings of the Fourteenth Conference on Computational Natural Language Learning — Shared Task*, pages 1–12.

Ken Hyland. 1998. *Hedging in scientific research articles*. John Benjamins B.V., Amsterdam, Netherlands.

Halil Kilicoglu and Sabine Bergler. 2008. Recognizing speculative language in biomedical research articles: a linguistically motivated perspective. *BMC Bioinformatics*, 9 Suppl 11:s10.

Halil Kilicoglu and Sabine Bergler. 2010. A High-Precision Approach to Detecting Hedges and Their Scopes. In *Proceedings of the Fourteenth Conference on Computational Natural Language Learning*, pages 70–77.

Halil Kilicoglu and Sabine Bergler. 2011. Effective Bio-Event Extraction using Trigger Words and Syntactic Dependencies. *Computational Intelligence*, 27(4):583–609.

Halil Kilicoglu. 2012. *Embedding Predications*. Ph.D. thesis, Concordia University.

Jin-Dong Kim, Tomoko Ohta, and Jun'ichi Tsujii. 2008. Corpus annotation for mining biomedical events from literature. *BMC Bioinformatics*, 9:10.

Jin-Dong Kim, Tomoko Ohta, Sampo Pyysalo, Yoshinobu Kano, and Jun'ichi Tsujii. 2009. Overview of BioNLP'09 Shared Task on Event Extraction. In *Proceedings of Natural Language Processing in Biomedicine (BioNLP) NAACL 2009 Workshop*, pages 1–9.

Jin-Dong Kim, Ngan Nguyen, Yue Wang, Jun'ichi Tsujii, Toshihisa Takagi, and Akinori Yonezawa. 2012. The Genia Event and Protein Coreference tasks of the BioNLP Shared Task 2011. *BMC Bioinformatics*, 13 Suppl 11:S1.

Marc Light, Xin Y. Qiu, and Padmini Srinivasan. 2004. The language of bioscience: facts, speculations, and statements in between. In *BioLINK 2004: Linking Biological Literature, Ontologies and Databases*, pages 17–24.

Christopher D. Manning, Mihai Surdeanu, John Bauer, Jenny Finkel, Steven J. Bethard, and David McClosky. 2014. The Stanford CoreNLP natural language processing toolkit. In *Proceedings of 52nd*

Annual Meeting of the Association for Computational Linguistics: System Demonstrations, pages 55–60.

Ben Medlock and Ted Briscoe. 2007. Weakly supervised learning for hedge classification in scientific literature. In *Proceedings of the 45th Meeting of the Association for Computational Linguistics*, pages 992–999.

Makoto Miwa, Paul Thompson, John McNaught, Douglas B. Kell, and Sophia Ananiadou. 2012. Extracting semantically enriched events from biomedical literature. *BMC Bioinformatics*, 13:108.

Roser Morante and Caroline Sporleder. 2012. Modality and negation: An introduction to the special issue. *Computational Linguistics*, 38(2):223–260.

Roser Morante, Vincent van Asch, and Walter Daelemans. 2010. Memory-based resolution of insentence scopes of hedge cues. In *Proceedings of the Fourteenth Conference on Computational Natural Language Learning*, pages 40–47.

Sergei Nirenburg and Victor Raskin. 2004. *Ontological Semantics*. The MIT Press, Cambridge, MA.

Roser Saurí and James Pustejovsky. 2009. FactBank: a corpus annotated with event factuality. *Language Resources and Evaluation*, 43(3):227–268.

Roser Saurí and James Pustejovsky. 2012. Are You Sure That This Happened? Assessing the Factuality Degree of Events in Text. *Computational Linguistics*, 38(2):261–299.

Roser Saurí. 2008. *A Factuality Profiler for Eventualities in Text*. Ph.D. thesis, Brandeis University.

Pontus Stenetorp, Sampo Pyysalo, Tomoko Ohta, Sophia Ananiadou, and Jun'ichi Tsujii. 2012. Bridging the gap between scope-based and event-based negation/speculation annotations: A bridge not too far. In *Proceedings of the Workshop on Extra-Propositional Aspects of Meaning in Computational Linguistics*, pages 47–56.

György Szarvas, Veronika Vincze, Richárd Farkas, György Móra, and Iryna Gurevych. 2012. Cross-genre and cross-domain detection of semantic uncertainty. *Computational Linguistics*, 38(2):335–367.

Paul Thompson, Raheel Nawaz, John McNaught, and Sophia Ananiadou. 2011. Enriching a biomedical event corpus with meta-knowledge annotation. *BMC Bioinformatics*, 12:393.

Özlem Uzuner, Imre Solti, and Eithon Cadag. 2010. Extracting medication information from clinical text. *JAMIA*, 17(5):514–518.

Veronika Vincze, György Szarvas, Richárd Farkas, György Móra, and János Csirik. 2008. The BioScope corpus: biomedical texts annotated for uncertainty, negation and their scopes. *BMC Bioinformatics*, 9 Suppl 11:S9.

W. John Wilbur, Andrey Rzhetsky, and Hagit Shatkay. 2006. New directions in biomedical text annotations: definitions, guidelines and corpus construction. *BMC Bioinformatics*, 7:356.

Committed Belief Tagging on the FactBank and LU Corpora: A Comparative Study

Gregory J. Werner
Department of Computer Science
George Washington University
Washington, DC, USA
gwerner@gwu.edu

Vinodkumar Prabhakaran
Department of Computer Science
Columbia University
New York, NY, USA
vinod@cs.columbia.edu

Mona Diab
Department of Computer Science
George Washington University
Washington, DC, USA
mtdiab@gwu.edu

Owen Rambow
Center for Computational Learning Systems
Columbia University
New York, NY, USA
rambow@ccls.columbia.edu

Abstract

Level of committed belief is a modality in natural language, it expresses a speak-er/writers belief in a proposition. Initial work exploring this phenomenon in the literature both from a linguistic and computational modeling perspective shows that it is a challenging phenomenon to capture, yet of great interest to several downstream NLP applications. In this work, we focus on identifying relevant features to the task of determining the level of committed belief tagging in two corpora specifically annotated for the phenomenon: the LU corpus and the FactBank corpus. We perform a thorough analysis comparing tagging schemes, infrastructure machinery, feature sets, preprocessing schemes and data genres and their impact on performance in both corpora. Our best results are an F1 score of 75.7 on the FactBank corpus and 72.9 on the smaller LU corpus.

1 Introduction

Level of Committed belief (LCB) is a linguistic modality expressing a speaker or writer's (SW) level of commitment to a given proposition, which could be their own or a reported proposition. Modeling this type of knowledge explicitly is useful in determining an SWs cognitive state, also referred to as person's private state (Wiebe et al., 2005). Wiebe et al. (2005) use the definition of (Quirk et al., 1985), who defines a private state to be an "internal (state) that cannot be directly observed by others". Determining the cognitive state of an SW can be relevant to several natural language processing (NLP) tasks such as question answering, information extraction, confidence determination in people's deduced opinions, determining the veracity of information, understanding power/influence relations in linguistic communication, etc. As an example, in (Rosenthal and McKeown, 2012), LCB was used to improve their claim detector which in turn allowed for improvements in influence prediction.

Initial work addressed the task of automatically identifying LCB of the SW. Approaches to date have relied on supervised models dependent on manually annotated data. There are two standard annotated corpora, the LU corpus (Diab et al., 2009) and FactBank (Saurí and Pustejovsky, 2009). Though in effect aiming for the same objective, both corpora use different terminology, different annotation standards, and they cover different genres. Previous studies performed on these corpora were conducted independently. In this work, we explore both corpora systematically and investigate their respective proposed tag sets. We experiment with multiple machine learning algorithms, varying the tag sets as we go along. Our goal is to build an automatic LCB tagger that is robust in a multi-genre context. Eventually we aim to adapt this tagger to other languages. The LCB tagging task aims at automatically identifying beliefs which can be ascribed to a SW, and at identifying the strength level by which

Proceedings of the Second Workshop on Extra-Propositional Aspects of Meaning in Computational Semantics (ExProM 2015), pages 32–40,
Denver, Colorado, June 5, 2015.

he or she holds them. Across languages, many different linguistic devices are used to denote this attitude towards an uttered proposition, including syntax, lexicon, and morphology. In this work we focus our investigation of LCB tagging in English and we only address the problem from the perspective of the SW. We do not address nested LCB where the SW is reporting the LCB of other people (leading to nested attributions, as done in FactBank following the MPQA Sentiment corpus (Wiebe et al., 2005).

2 Background

Initial work on LCB was undertaken by Diab et al. (2009), who built the LU corpus that contains belief annotations for propositional heads in text. They used a 3-way distinction of belief tags: Committed Belief (CB) where the SW strongly believes in the proposition, Non-committed belief (NCB) where the SW reflects a weak belief in the proposition, and Non Attributable Belief (NA) where the SW is not (or could not be) expressing a belief in the proposition (e.g., desires, questions etc.). The LU corpus comprises over 13,000 word tokens from sixteen documents covering four genres: 9 newswire documents, 4 training manuals, 2 correspondences and 1 interview. One of the issues with this annotation scheme is that the annotations for NCB conflate the cases where the SW explicitly conveys the weakness of belief (e.g., using modal auxiliaries such as may) and the cases where the SW is reporting someone else's belief about a proposition. In this paper, we tease apart these original NCB cases and arrive at a 4-way belief distinction using the original annotations in the LU corpus (details to be discussed in Section 3.1).

The LCB tagger developed using the original LU corpus (Prabhakaran et al., 2010) obtained a best performance (64% F-measure) using the Yamcha[1] machine learning framework which leverages Support Vector Machines in a supervised manner, and a performance of 59% F-measure using the Conditional Random Fields (CRF) algorithm. Their experiments were limited in scope because the LU Corpus is fairly small. This led to an under-representation of NCB tags in the training corpus and a relatively shallow understanding of how LCB tagging performs across genres. In this paper, we perform a detailed investigation through extensive machine learning experiments to understand how the size of data and genre variations affect the performance of an LCB tagger. We also systematically measure the impact of augmenting the training data with more data as well as measuring performance differences when the training data comprises a single genre vs. multiple genres. It should be noted that although we experiment with similar machine learning frameworks, our results are not directly comparable since the Prabhakaran et al. (2010) work applied cross validation to the LU-3 corpus, while we did not follow the same experimental strategy. Additionally, in this work we use a lot more features than those reported in the previous study.

A closely related corpus is FactBank (FB; Saurí and Pustejovsky (2009)), which captures factuality annotations on top of event annotations in TimeML. FactBank is annotated on the genre of newswire. FactBank models the factuality of events at three levels: certain (CT), probable (PB) and possible (PS), and distinguishes the polarity (e.g., CT- means certainly not true). Moreover it marks an unknown category (Uu), which refers to uncommitted or underspecified belief. It also captures the source of the factuality assertions, thereby distinguishing the SW's factuality assertions from those of a source introduced by the author. Despite the terminology difference between FactBank ("factuality") and LU ("committed belief"), they both address the same type of linguistic modality phenomenon namely level of committed belief. Accordingly, with the appropriate mapping, both corpora can be used in conjunction to model LCB. From a computational perspective, FactBank differs from the LU corpus in two major respects (other than the granularity in which they capture annotations): 1) FactBank is roughly four times the size of the LU corpus, and 2) FactBank is more homogeneous in terms of genre than the LU corpus as it consists primarily of newswire. In this paper, we unify the factuality annotations in Factback and the level of committed belief annotations present in the LU corpus to a 4-way committed-belief distinction.[2]

[1]http://chasen.org/~taku/software/yamcha/

[2]For an additional discussion of the relation between factuality and belief, see (Prabhakaran et al., 2015)

3 Approach

Following previous work (Prabhakaran et al., 2010), we adopt a supervised approach to the LCB problem. We experiment with the two available manually annotated corpora, the LU and FB corpora. Going beyond previous approaches to the problem reported in the literature, our goal is to create a robust LCB system while gaining a deeper understanding of the phenomenon of LCB as an expressed modality by systematically teasing apart the different factors that affect performance.

3.1 Annotation Transformations

The NCB category of the LU tagging scheme captures two different notions: that of uncertainty of the speaker/writer and that of belief being attributed to someone other than the SW. Accordingly, we manually split the NCB into the NCB tag and the Reported Belief tag (ROB). Reported belief is the case where the SW's intention is to report on someone else's stated belief, whether or not they themselves believe it. An example of this would be the sentence *John said he studies everyday*. While the 'say' proposition is an example of committed belief (CB) on the part of the SW, the SW makes no assertion about the 'study' proposition attributed to John, and therefore *studies* is labeled ROB. This relabeling of the NCB tag into NCB and ROB was carried out manually by co-authors Werner and Rambow, who are native speakers of English. The inter-annotator agreement was 93%. The cases where there were contentions were discussed and an adjudication process was followed where a single annotation was agreed upon. This was a relatively fast process since the number of NCB annotated data is very small in the original LU corpus (176 instances). This conversion resulted in the LU-4 corpus designating the fact that this version of the LU corpus is a 4-way annotated corpus. This is in contrast to the original version of LU corpus with the 3-way distinction, LU-3.

To illustrate the difference between each of the tags in the LU-4 corpus, we provide a few examples from the annotated corpus. The sentence 1 shows the contrast between the committed belief in the author knowing and the non-committed belief in the author being uncertain of it (a flu vaccine) working. The other two tags are demonstrated in the sentence 2 where the author is saying Reed accused however Reed is the one talking about failing and not the author. To contrast we note that although Reed is attributed the notion of failing, neither the author nor Reed demonstrate any belief of the verb to probe and therefore it is not-attributable to any source mentioned in this sentence.

(1) But we only <CB> know </CB> that it might <NCB> work </NCB> because of laboratory studies and animal studies uh uh

(2) Democratic leader Harry Reed <CB> accused </CB> Republicans of <ROB> failing </ROB> to <NA> probe </NA> allegations ...

In order to render the FactBank (FB) corpus comparable to the LU-4 corpus, we mapped tags in the FB corpus into the 4-way tag scheme adopted in the LU-4 framework. Accordingly, we mapped CT directly into CB, PB and PS directly into NCB, and Uu was mapped into either NA or ROB. We used the number and identity of sources to determine if the Uu of FB was due to belief expressed by a source other than the SW. Specifically, if the same proposition is marked Uu for the SW, but the annotations also capture factuality attributed to another source, then we conclude the tag should be ROB. If there is no other attribution on the proposition other than the Uu attributed to the SW, we consider the tag to be NA. We refer to the resulting version of the FB corpus as FB-4. It is worth noting that because the genre of the FB corpus is newswire, it has a relatively large number of ROB annotations. Moreover, FB explicitly marks LCB with respect to various nested sources. However in our mapping, we only consider the annotations from the perspective of the SW.

We give a few examples of the original FactBank work as to compare and contrast the notion of belief carried in each corpus. In sentence 3, we have clear cut mapping between the certainty of the author in think and committed belief. Likewise, doing is a non-committed belief. In each case, the polarity is discarded in our transformations. The sentence 4 reveals the case where teaches takes on a reported belief meaning as it is given both a certain tag for the school and an unknown tag for the author. An example where Uu does not constitute reported belief is shown in the sentence 5, where only one entity's belief is conveyed, and that is of the author.

(3) ... Yeah I <CT+> think </CT+> he's <PR+> doing </PR> the right thing

(4) The school <CT+> says </CT+> it <CT+> <Uu> teaches </Uu> </CT+> the children to be good Muslims and good students.

(5) I <CT+> urge <CT+> you to <Uu> do <Uu> the right thing ...

The tag distribution breakdown in the corpora is illustrated in Table 1.

	CB	NCB	ROB	NA	Total
LU-3	631	176		589	13485
LU-4	631	15	161	589	13485
FB-4	3837	156	2074	661	82845

Table 1: Label distribution in the LU-3, LU-4 and FB-4 corpora.

3.2 Experimental Set Up

3.2.1 Corpus Combination

We experiment with the three corpora LU-3 (with the labels CB, NCB and NA), LU-4 and FB-4 (each with the labels CB, NCB, NA, and ROB). We present results on each of the corpora and their combinations for training and testing. In general we split our corpora at the sentence level into training and test sets with 5/6 for training and 1/6 for test by reserving every sixth sentence for the test set.

3.2.2 Features

We use a number of features proposed by Prabhakaran et al. (2010), as well as a few more recent additions, and we hold them constant across our different experimental conditions. This feature set comprises the following base set of lexical and syntactic based features. *General Features* for each token include its lemma, part of speech (POS), as well as the lemma and POS of two preceding and following tokens. *Dependency features* include sibling's lemma, sibling's POS, child's lemma, child's POS, parent's lemma, parent's POS, ancestors' lemmas, ancestor's POS, reporting ancestor's POS, reporting ancestor's lemma, dependency relationship

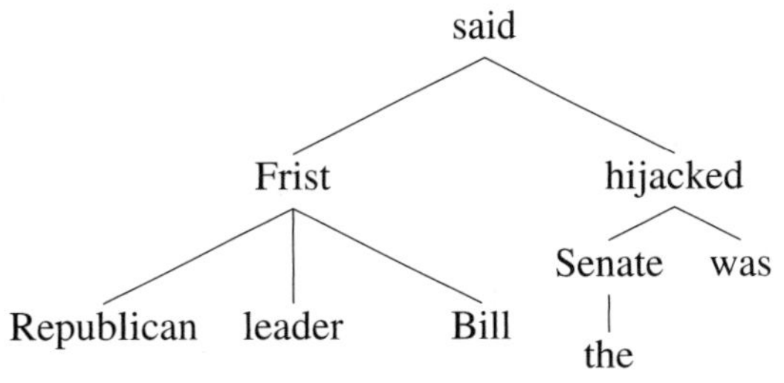

Figure 1: Dependency tree for example sentence.

and lemma of the closest ancestor whose POS is a noun, dependency relationship and lemma of the closest ancestor whose POS is a verb, token under the scope of a conditional (*if/when*), ancestor under the scope of a conditional (*if/when*). We use the Dependency Parser provided in the Stanford NLP toolkit. A pictorial explanation of some of these dependency features is given in Figure 1 and Table 2 for the sentence "Republican leader Bill Frist said the Senate was hijacked".

Feature Name	Value
PosTag	VBN
Lemma	hijack
WhichModalAmI	nil
UnderConditional	N/A
AncestorUnderConditional	N/A
FirstDepAncestorofPos	{hijack, NIL}, {say, ccomp}
DepAncestors	{say,VBD}
Siblings	{Frist, NNP}
Parent	{say, VBD, say-37.7-1}
Child	{Senate, NNP}, {be, VBD}
DepRel	{ccomp}

Table 2: Representative features for the token hijacked in the example sentence.

3.2.3 Machine Learning Infrastructure

We experiment with five machine learning algorithms. A. Conditional Random Fields (CRF) to allow for comparison with previous work; B. Linear Support Vector Machines (LSVM); C. Quadratic Kernel Support Vector Machines (QSVM); D. Naive Bayes (NB); and, E. Logistic Regression (LREG). We provide NB as a generative contrast to the discriminative SVM and CRF methods. Moreover,

QSVM quite often yields better results at the expense of longer runtime, hence, we explore if that is the case within the LCB task.

The parameters for each of the five algorithms are held constant across all experiments and not tuned for specific configurations. The notable parameters that are used are listed in Table 3.

Algorithm	Notable Parameters
CRF	Gaussian Variance=10, Orders = 1, Iterations = 500
LSVM	Linear Kernel (t=0), Classification (z=c), Cost Factor (j=1), Biased Hyperplane (b=1), Do not remove inconsistent training examples (i=0)
QSVM	Polynomial Kernel (t=1), Quadratic (d=1), Classification (z=c), Cost Factor (j=1), Biased Hyperplane (b=1), Do not remove inconsistent training examples (i=0)
NB	Default
LREG	Default

Table 3: Parameter settings per algorithm.

3.2.4 Tools

A list of major NLP tools used is illustrated in Table 4. We used the CoreNLP pipeline for tokenization, sentence splitting, part of speech determination, lemmatization, named entity recognition, dependency parsing and coreference resolution. ClearTK provided us easy access to the machine learning algorithms we used which includes SVM Light for both SVM kernels and Mallet for CRF. It also provides us the backbone for our annotation structure.

4 Experiments

4.1 Evaluation metric

We ran 30 experiments, which are all the possible permutations of the three variables, listed above: do we split the NCB tag into 2 tags, what corpora do we train on, and what machine learning algorithm do we use. We report results using the overall weighted micro average F1 score.

Name	Source	Ver.
CoreNLP	(Manning et al., 2014)	3.5
ClearTK	(Bethard et al., 2014)	2.0
UIMA	https://uima.apache.org/	2.6
uimaFIT	(Ogren and Bethard, 2009)	2.1
Mallet	(McCallum, 2002)	2.0.7
SVM Light	(Joachims, 1999)	6.0.2

Table 4: NLP Tools Used.

4.2 Condition 1: Impact of splitting NCB tag in the LU corpus

We show the overall impact of splitting the NCB tag in the original LU corpus into two tags: NCB and ROB. The training and test corpora are from the same corpus, i.e. training and test sets are from LU-3 or LU-4. The results are reported on the respective test sets using the F1 score. The hypothesis is that a 4-way tagging scheme should result in better overall scores if the tagging scheme indeed captures a more genuine explicit representation for LCB. Table 5 illustrates the results yielded from the 5 ML algorithms. We note that the 4-way tagging outperforms the 3-way tagging for CRF and LSVM, however, the NB algorithm doesn't seem as sensitive to the tagging scheme (3 vs. 4 tags), and QSVM and LREG seem to be better performing in the 3 tag setting than the 4 tag setting. This might be a result of the number of tags in the 4-way tagging scheme breaking up the space for NCB's considerably. Overall the highest score is obtained by LSVM (72.89 F1 score) for LU-4, namely in the 4-way tagging scheme, suggesting that a 4-way split of the annotation space is an appropriate level of annotation granularity.

4.3 Condition 2: Impact of size and corpus genre homogeneity on LCB performance

In this condition we attempt to tease apart the impact of corpus size (FB being 4 times the size of the LU corpus) as well as corpus homogeneity, since FB is relatively homogeneous in genre compared to the LU corpus. Similar to Condition 1, we show the results yielded by all 5 ML algorithms. Results are reported in Table 6. Our hypothesis is that the overall results obtained on the FB should outper-

Test Set	Algorithm	Overall F-score
LU-4	CRF	71.33
LU-4	**LSVM**	**72.89**
LU-4	QSVM	68.10
LU-4	NB	61.61
LU-4	LREG	70.75
LU-3	CRF	68.25
LU-3	LSVM	69.77
LU-3	QSVM	69.21
LU-3	NB	61.58
LU-3	**LREG**	**71.26**

Table 5: Condition 1: LU-3 and LU-4 results using micro average F1 score on their respective test data.

Test Set	Algorithm	Overall F-score
FB-4	CRF	73.34
FB-4	LSVM	74.36
FB-4	**QSVM**	**75.57**
FB-4	NB	66.22
FB-4	LREG	74.67
LU-4	CRF	71.33
LU-4	**LSVM**	**72.89**
LU-4	QSVM	68.10
LU-4	NB	61.61
LU-4	LREG	70.75

Table 6: Condition 2: FB-4 and LU-4 results using micro average F1 score on their respective test data.

form those obtained on the LU corpus. Note that the results in the Table 6 are not directly comparable across corpora since the test sets are different: each experimental condition is tested within the same corpus, i.e. FB-4 is trained using FB-4 training data and tested on FB-4 test data, and LU-4 is trained using LU-4 training data and tested on LU-4 test data. However, the results validate our hypothesis that more data which is more homogeneous results in a better LCB tagger.

It is noted that the various ML algorithms perform differently for LU-4 vs. FB-4. In order, for FB-4, QSVM outperforms LREG which in turn outperforms LSVM, CRF and NB. In contrast, for LU the LSVM is the best performing ML algorithm followed by CRF, QSVM, LREG, and finally NB. The linear kernel SVM, LSVM, has the closest performance between the two, yet the difference is still statistically significant.

A deeper analysis on each of the four tags shows a remarkable difference in F1-measure for reported belief (ROB) for the two corpora as illustrated in Table 7. ROB is significantly better identified in the FB-4 corpus compared to the LU-4 corpus. This is expected since the FB-4 corpus has significantly more ROB tags in the training data. The number of ROB tags in training sets for LU-4 is 100 and for FB-4 it is 1800. The NA tag on the other hand performs better in the LU-4 corpus than in the FB-4 as seen in Table 8. The number of NA tags in the LU-4 training data is 460, while in the FB-4 training data (which is much larger) there are 600. In the case of FB-4 they only constitute a small percentage of the overall data compared to their percentage in the LU-4 corpus.

Test Set	Algorithm	P	R	F
LU-4	**CRF**	**66.67**	**40.00**	**50.00**
LU-4	LSVM	39.13	45.00	41.86
LU-4	QSVM	50.00	15.00	23.08
LU-4	NB	0.00	0.00	0.00
LU-4	LREG	41.67	25.00	31.25
FB-4	CRF	76.79	73.22	74.97
FB-4	LSVM	76.08	72.13	74.05
FB-4	**QSVM**	**72.86**	**79.23**	**75.92**
FB-4	NB	57.27	67.76	62.08
FB-4	LREG	74.59	73.77	74.18

Table 7: ROB results in FB-4 and LU-4 Corpora.

Test Set	Algorithm	P	R	F
LU-4	CRF	70.59	77.42	73.85
LU-4	**LSVM**	**80.21**	**82.80**	**81.48**
LU-4	QSM	64.91	79.57	71.50
LU-4	NB	66.32	67.74	67.02
LU-4	LREG	76.00	81.72	78.76
FB-4	CRF	52.38	44.72	48.25
FB-4	LSVM	50.74	56.10	53.28
FB-4	**QSVM**	**61.76**	**51.22**	**56.00**
FB-4	NB	0.00	0.00	0.00
FB-4	LREG	54.63	47.97	51.08

Table 8: NA results in FB-4 and LU-4 corpora.

4.4 Condition 3: Measuring impact of training data size on performance: combining training FB-4 and LU-4 data

In this condition, we wanted to investigate the impact of training using the combined FB-4 and LU-4 training corpora on 3 test sets: LU-4 Test, FB-4 Test and LU-4 Test + FB-4 Test. A reasonable hypothesis is that, with a larger corpus created by combining the two individual corpora we will see better results on any test corpus. Table 9 illustrates the experimental results for this condition where the training data for both corpora are combined.

The worst overall results are obtained on the LU-4 test set, while the best are obtained on the FB-4 test set. This is expected since the size of the training data coming from the FB-4 corpus overwhelms that of the LU corpus and the LU corpus is relatively diverse in genre, potentially adding noise. Also we note that the results on the LU-4 corpus are much worse than the results obtained and illustrated in Table 5 when the training data was significantly smaller, yet of strictly the same genre of the test data. This observation seems to suggest that homogeneity between training and test data for the LCB task trumps training data size. We also note that this observation is furthermore supported by the slight degradation in performance in the FB-4 test set compared to the performance results reported in Table 6 for the ML algorithms CRF and QSVM. However, we observe that LREG, NB and LSVM each was able to generalize better from the augmented data when additionally using the LU-4 training data, but the improvements were relatively insignificant (less than 1%). This may be attributed to the addition of the LU-4 training data, which adds noise to the LCB training task leading to inconclusive results. Testing on a combined corpus shows that LREG algorithm yields the best results.

Test Set	Algorithm	Overall F-score
LU-4	CRF	56.30
LU-4	**LSVM**	**61.10**
LU-4	QSVM	58.05
LU-4	NB	45.32
LU-4	LREG	59.90
FB-4	CRF	73.02
FB-4	LSVM	74.99
FB-4	QSVM	75.00
FB-4	NB	67.37
FB-4	**LREG**	**75.23**
FB-4 + LU-4	CRF	70.47
FB-4 + LU-4	LSVM	72.85
FB-4 + LU-4	QSVM	72.48
FB-4 + LU-4	NB	64.02
FB-4 + LU-4	**LREG**	**72.88**

Table 9: Condition 3: Micro average F1 score results obtained on three sets of test data while trained using a combination of FB-4 and LU-4 training data.

4.5 Condition 4: Machine Learning Algorithm Performance

From the first three conditions, we are able to conclude how reliably certain machine learning algorithms outperform others. In our research, we have mainly focused on SVM Light's linear kernel (LSVM) and expect it to perform quite well. Certainly, we would expect it to outperform the CRFs, as they did in previous work. Changing the linear kernel to a quadratic kernel might give us some improvement at the expense of training time since it takes much longer to complete. Our intuition as far as CRFs being outperformed by SVMs seem to hold uniformly as Tables 5, 6 and 9 illustrate. To augment the linear kernel SVM, the quadratic kernel only gives an improvement in some cases.

The NB models performed predictably poorly. Surprisingly, the LREG models appear to be robust, with performance that is comparable to the best SVM models (LSVM and QSVM) in our experiments. In fact, for the FB-4 case, LREG performed slightly better than either LSVM or QSVM. Given the efficiency of LREG in terms of training and testing, and its comparable performance to SVMs, using LREG for feature exploration in the context of LCB tagging makes it a very attractive ML framework to tune parameters with, keeping the more sophisticated ML algorithms for final testing.

Sometimes it is other components that cause an error. Take this example sentence from the LSVM algorithm acting on the LU corpus: It also checks on guard posts. Checks has been annotated CB and correctly so by the human involved. The tagger marks checks as O, or lacking author belief, because the token checks has been labeled a noun by the part-of-speech checker. A more proper miss can be found on the sentence You know what's sort of interesting Paula once again taken from the LU corpus. Although labeled as NA, the token know is labeled as CB. Since it has the feel of a question the annotator has stated that there is no committed belief on the part of the author. This is one that the algorithm itself has clearly gotten wrong. The CRF on the same sentence chose O, or lack of belief. NB got the token correct. LREG chose O. QSVM took the same approach as the LSVM labeling it as CB. This illustration shows the worse performing algorithm on the LU-4 corpus being the only correct answer showing perhaps that detecting phrases and sentences formed as questions are harder to analyze.

5 Conclusions

The results suggest that 4-way LCB tagging is an appropriate LCB granularity level. Training and testing on the FB-4 corpus results in overall better performance than training and testing on the LU corpus. We have seen that the LCB task is quite sensitive to the consistency in genre across training and test data, and that more out-of-genre data is not always the best route to overall performance improvement. SVMs were one of the best performing ML platforms in the context of this task as well as Logistic regression.

Acknowledgements

This paper is based upon work supported by the DARPA DEFT Program. The views expressed are those of the authors and do not reflect the official policy or position of the Department of Defense or the U.S. Government. We also thank the anonymous reviewers for their constructive feedback.

References

Steven Bethard, Philip Ogren, and Lee Becker. 2014. ClearTK 2.0: Design Patterns for Machine Learning in UIMA. In *Proceedings of the Ninth International Conference on Language Resources and Evaluation (LREC'14)*, pages 3289–3293, Reykjavik, Iceland, 5. European Language Resources Association (ELRA).

Mona Diab, Lori Levin, Teruko Mitamura, Owen Rambow, Vinodkumar Prabhakaran, and Weiwei Guo. 2009. Committed Belief Annotation and Tagging. In *Proceedings of the Third Linguistic Annotation Workshop*, pages 68–73, Suntec, Singapore, August.

Thorsten Joachims. 1999. Making Large-Scale SVM Learning Practical. In Bernhard Schölkopf, Christopher J.C. Burges, and A. Smola, editors, *Advances in Kernel Methods - Support Vector Learning*, Cambridge, MA, USA. MIT Press.

Christopher D. Manning, Mihai Surdeanu, John Bauer, Jenny Finkel, Steven J. Bethard, and David McClosky. 2014. The Stanford CoreNLP Natural Language Processing Toolkit. In *Proceedings of 52nd Annual Meeting of the Association for Computational Linguistics: System Demonstrations*, pages 55–60, Baltimore, Maryland, June.

Andrew Kachites McCallum. 2002. MALLET: A Machine Learning for Language Toolkit. http://www.cs.umass.edu/ mccallum/mallet.

Philip Ogren and Steven Bethard. 2009. Building Test Suites for UIMA Components. In *Proceedings of the Workshop on Software Engineering, Testing, and Quality Assurance for Natural Language Processing (SETQA-NLP 2009)*, pages 1–4, Boulder, Colorado, June.

Vinodkumar Prabhakaran, Owen Rambow, and Mona Diab. 2010. Automatic Committed Belief Tagging. In *Coling 2010: Posters*, pages 1014–1022, Beijing, China, August. Coling 2010 Organizing Committee.

Vinodkumar Prabhakaran, Tomas By, Julia Hirschberg, Owen Rambow, Samira Shaikh, Tomek Strzalkowski,

Jennifer Tracey, Michael Arrigo, Rupayan Basu, Micah Clark, Adam Dalton, Mona Diab, Louise Guthrie, Anna Prokofieva, Stephanie Strassel, Gregory Werner, Janyce Wiebe, and Yorick Wilks. 2015. A New Dataset and Evaluation for Belief/Factuality. In *Proceedings of the Fourth Joint Conference on Lexical and Computational Semantics (*SEM 2015)*, Denver, USA, June.

Randolph Quirk, Sidney Greenbaum, Geoffrey Leech, and Jan Svartvik. 1985. *A Comprehensive Grammar of the English Language*. Longman, London.

Sara Rosenthal and Kathleen McKeown. 2012. Detecting Opinionated Claims in Online Discussions. In *Semantic Computing (ICSC), 2012 IEEE Sixth International Conference on*, pages 30–37. IEEE.

Roser Saurí and James Pustejovsky. 2009. FactBank: A Corpus Annotated with Event Factuality. *Language Resources and Evaluation*, 43:227–268. 10.1007/s10579-009-9089-9.

Janyce Wiebe, Theresa Wilson, and Claire Cardie. 2005. Annotating Expressions of Opinions and Emotions in Language. *Language Resources and Evaluation*, 39(2-3):165–210.

Extending NegEx with Kernel Methods for Negation Detection in Clinical Text

Chaitanya Shivade[†], Marie-Catherine de Marneffe[§], Eric Fosler-Lussier[†], Albert M. Lai[*]
[†]Department of Computer Science and Engineering,
[§]Department of Linguistics,
[*]Department of Biomedical Informatics,
The Ohio State University, Columbus OH 43210, USA.
shivade@cse.ohio-state.edu, mcdm@ling.ohio-state.edu
fosler@cse.ohio-state.edu, albert.lai@osumc.edu

Abstract

NegEx is a popular rule-based system used to identify negated concepts in clinical notes. This system has been reported to perform very well by numerous studies in the past. In this paper, we demonstrate the use of kernel methods to extend the performance of NegEx. A kernel leveraging the rules of NegEx and its output as features, performs as well as the rule-based system. An improvement in performance is achieved if this kernel is coupled with a bag of words kernel. Our experiments show that kernel methods outperform the rule-based system, when evaluated within and across two different open datasets. We also present the results of a semi-supervised approach to the problem, which improves performance on the data.

1 Introduction

Clinical narratives consisting of free-text documents are an important part of the electronic medical record (EMR). Medical professionals often need to search the EMR for notes corresponding to specific medical events for a particular patient. Recruitment of subjects in research studies such as clinical trials involves searching through the EMR of multiple patients to find a cohort of relevant candidates. Most information retrieval approaches determine a document to be relevant to a concept based on the presence of that concept in the document. However, these approaches fall short if these concepts are negated, leading to a number of false positives. This is an important problem especially in the clinical domain. For example, the sentence: "The scan showed no signs of malignancy" has the concept 'malignancy' which was looked for in the patient, but was not observed to be present. The task of negation detection is to identify whether a given concept is negated or affirmed in a sentence. NegEx (Chapman et al., 2001) is a rule-based system developed to detect negated concepts in the clinical domain and has been extensively used in the literature.

In this paper, we show that a kernel-based approach can map this rule-based system into a machine learning system and extends its performance. We validate the generalization capabilities of our approach by evaluating it across datasets. Finally, we demonstrate that a semi-supervised approach can also achieve an improvement over the baseline rule-based system, a valuable finding in the clinical domain where annotated data is expensive to generate.

2 Related Work

Negation has been a popular research topic in the medical domain in recent years. NegEx (Chapman et al., 2001) along with its extensions (South et al., 2006; Chapman et al., 2013) is one of the oldest and most widely used negation detection system because of its simplicity and speed. An updated version - ConText (Harkema et al., 2009) was also released to incorporate features such as temporality and experiencer identification, in addition to negation. These algorithms are designed using simple rules that fire based on the presence of particular cues, before and after the concept. However, as with all rule-based systems, they lack generalization. Shortage of training data discouraged the use of machine learning techniques in clinical natural language processing

Proceedings of the Second Workshop on Extra-Propositional Aspects of Meaning in Computational Semantics (ExProM 2015), pages 41–46,
Denver, Colorado, June 5, 2015.

(NLP) in the past. However, shared tasks (Uzuner et al., 2011) and other recent initiatives (Albright et al., 2013) are making more clinical data available. This should be leveraged to harness the benefits offered by machine learning solutions. Recently, Wu et al. (2014) argued that negation detection is not of practical value without in-domain training and/or development, and described an SVM-based approach using hand-crafted features.

3 Kernel Methods

Our approach uses kernel methods to extend the abilities of the NegEx system. A kernel is a similarity function K, that maps two inputs x and y from a given domain into a similarity score that is a real number (Hofmann et al., 2008). Formally, it is a function $K(x, y) = \langle\phi(x), \phi(y)\rangle \rightarrow R$, where $\phi(x)$ is some feature function over instance x. For a function K to be a valid kernel, it should be symmetric and positive-semidefinite. In this section, we describe the different kernels we implemented for the task of negation detection.

3.1 NegEx Features Kernel

The source code of NegEx[1] reveals rules using three sets of negation cues. These are termed as pseudo negation phrases, negation phrases and post negation phrases. Apart from these cues, the system also looks for a set of conjunctions in a sentence. We used the source code of the rule-based system and constructed a binary feature corresponding to each cue and conjunction, and thus generated a feature vector for every sentence in the dataset. Using the LibSVM (Chang and Lin, 2011) implementation, we constructed a linear kernel which we refer to as the NegEx Features Kernel (NF).

3.2 Augmented Bag of Words Kernel

We also designed a kernel that augmented with bag of words the decision by NegEx. For each dataset, we constructed a binary feature vector for every sentence. This vector is comprised of two parts, a vector indicating presence or absence of every word in that dataset and augment it with a single feature indicating the output of the NegEx rule-based system. We did not filter stop-words since many stop-words serve as cues for negated assertions. The idea behind constructing such a kernel was to allow the model to learn relative weighting of the NegEx output and the bag of words in the dataset. Again, a linear kernel using LibSVM was constructed: the Augmented Bag of Words Kernel (ABoW).

4 Datasets

A test set of de-identified sentences, extracted from clinical notes at the University of Pittsburgh Medical Center, is also available with the NegEx source code. In each sentence, a concept of interest has been annotated by physicians with respect to being negated or affirmed in the sentence. The concepts are non numeric clinical conditions (such as symptoms, findings and diseases) extracted from six types of clinical notes (e.g., discharge summaries, operative notes, echo-cardiograms).

The 2010 i2b2 challenge (Uzuner et al., 2011) on relation extraction had assertion classification as a subtask. The corpus for this task along with the annotations is freely available for download.[2] Based on a given target concept, participants had to classify assertions as either present, absent, or possible in the patient, conditionally present in the patient under certain circumstances, hypothetically present in the patient at some future point, and mentioned in the patient report but associated with someone other than the patient. Since we focus on negation detection, we selected only assertions corresponding to the positive and negative classes from the five assertion classes in the corpus, which simulates the type of data found in the NegEx Corpus. The i2b2 corpus has training data, partitioned into discharge summaries from Partners Healthcare (PH) and the Beth Israel Deaconess (BID) Medical Center. This gave us datasets from two more medical institutions. The corpus also has a test set, but does not have a split corresponding to these institutions.

Using the above corpora we constructed five datasets: 1) The dataset available with the NegEx rule-based system, henceforth referred to as the NegCorp dataset; 2) We adapted the training set of the i2b2 assertion classification task for negation detection, the i2b2Train$_{mod}$ dataset; 3) The training subset of i2b2Train$_{mod}$ from Partners Health-

[1] From https://code.google.com/p/NegEx/

[2] From https://www.i2b2.org/NLP/DataSets/

Dataset	Affirmed	Negated	Total
NegCorp	1885	491	2376
i2b2Train$_{mod}$	4476	1533	6009
PH subset	(1862)	(635)	(2497)
BID subset	(2614)	(898)	(3512)
i2b2Test$_{mod}$	8618	2594	11212

Table 1: Number of affirmed and negated concepts in each dataset.

care, henceforth referred to as the PH dataset; 4) The training subset of i2b2Train$_{mod}$ from the Beth Israel Deaconess Medical Center, henceforth referred to as the BID dataset; and 5) The adapted test set of the 2010 i2b2 challenge, henceforth referred to as the i2b2Test$_{mod}$ dataset. Table 1 summarizes the distribution for number of affirmed and negated assertions in each dataset.

5 Experiments

We implemented the kernels outlined in Section 3 and evaluated them within different datasets using precision, recall and F1 on ten-fold cross validation. We compared the performance of each model against the NegEx rule-based system as baseline.

5.1 Within dataset evaluation

As can be seen in Table 2, the NegEx Features Kernel performed similarly to the baseline (the improvement is not significant). However, the ABoW kernel significantly outperformed the baseline ($p<0.05$, McNemar's test). Joachims et al. (2001) showed that given two kernels K1 and K2, the composite kernel $K(x,y) = K1(x,y) + K2(x,y)$ is also a kernel. We constructed a composite kernel adding the kernel matrices for the ABoW and NF kernels, which resulted in a further (but not significant) improvement.

5.2 Cross dataset evaluation

In order to test the generalizability of our approach, we evaluated the performance of the ABoW kernel against the baseline. We trained the ABoW kernel on different datasets and tested them on the i2b2Test$_{mod}$ dataset. Table 3 summarizes the results of these experiments.

	Datasets		
System	NegCorp	BID	PH
NegEx (baseline)	94.6	84.2	87.3
NF Kernel	95.6	87.3	87.5
ABoW Kernel	**97.0**	**90.6**	**89.9**
ABoW+ NF Kernel	**97.3**	**92.4**	**91.3**

Table 2: Within dataset performance of kernels based on F1-score using 10-fold cross validation. Bold results indicate significant improvements over the baseline ($p<0.05$, McNemar's test).

System	Precision	Recall	F1
NegEx (baseline)	89.6	79.9	84.5
ABoW trained on			
NegCorp	89.9	79.3	84.2
PH	89.4	**88.1**	**88.7**
BID	89.2	**89.9**	**89.7**
i2b2Train$_{mod}$	89.9	**90.0**	**90.0**

Table 3: Cross dataset performance on the i2b2Test$_{mod}$ dataset given different training datasets.

We found that the ABoW kernel significantly outperformed the baseline when trained on datasets that were generated from the same corpus, namely PH and BID. A kernel trained on i2b2Train$_{mod}$, i.e., combining the PH and BID datasets performs better than the individually trained datasets. These experiments also tested the effect of training data size (PH $<$ BID $<$ i2b2Train$_{mod}$) on the kernel performance. We observed that the performance of the kernel increases as the size of the training data increases, though not significantly. The kernel trained on a dataset from a different corpus (NegCorp) performs as well as the baseline.

5.3 Semi-supervised approach

We tried a semi-supervised approach to train the ABoW kernel, which we tested on the i2b2Test$_{mod}$ dataset. We trained a kernel on the NegCorp dataset and recorded the predictions. We refer to these labels as "pseudo labels" in contrast to the gold labels of the i2b2Train$_{mod}$ dataset. We then trained a semi-supervised ABoW kernel, ABoW$_{ss}$ on the i2b2Train$_{mod}$ dataset to learn the pseudo labels for this predicted dataset. Finally, we tested ABoW_{ss} on the i2b2Test_{mod} dataset. Table 4 summarizes the results of these experiments. For ease of comparison, we restate the results of the ABoW kernel, ABoW_{gold} trained on the gold labels of the i2b2Train_{mod} dataset.

System	Precision	Recall	F1
NegEx	89.6	79.9	84.5
ABoW_{ss}	89.7	**82.1**	**85.7**
ABoW_{gold}	89.9	**90.0**	**90.0**

Table 4: Semi-supervised models on the i2b2Test_{mod} dataset.

These results demonstrate that the kernel trained using a semi-supervised approach performs better than the baseline ($p<0.05$, McNemar's test), but performs worse than a kernel trained using supervised training. However, supervised training is dependent on gold annotations. Thus, the semi-supervised approach achieves good results without the need for annotated data. This is an important result especially in the clinical domain where available annotated data is sparse and extremely costly to generate.

6 Dependency Tree Kernels

Dependency tree kernels have been showed to be effective for NLP tasks in the past. Culotta et al. (2004) showed that although tree kernels by themselves may not be effective for relation extraction, combining a tree kernel with a bag of words kernel showed promising results. Dependency tree kernels have also been explored in the context of negation extraction in the medical domain. Recently, Bowei et al. (2013) demonstrated the use of tree kernel based approaches in detecting the scope of negations and speculative sentences using the BioScope corpus (Szarvas et al., 2008). However, the task of negation scope detection task is different than that of negation detection. Among other differences, an important one being the presence of annotations for negation cues in the Bioscope corpus. Sohn et al. (2012) developed hand crafted rules representing subtrees of dependency parses of negated sentences and showed that they were effective on a dataset from their institution.

Therefore, we implemented a dependency tree kernel similar to the approach described in Culotta and Sorensen (2004) to automatically capture the structural patterns in negated assertions. We used the Stanford dependencies parser (version 2.0.4) (de Marneffe et al., 2006) to get the dependency parse for every assertion. As per their representation (de Marneffe and Manning, 2008) every dependency is a triple, consisting of a governor, a dependent and a dependency relation. In this triple, the governor and dependent are words from the input sentence. Thus, the tree kernel comprised of nodes corresponding to every word and every dependency relation in the parse. Node similarity was computed based on features such as lemma, generalized part-of-speech, WordNet (Fellbaum, 1998) synonymy and the UMLS (Bodenreider, 2004) semantic type obtained using MetaMap (Aronson, 2001) for word nodes.

Node similarity for dependency relation nodes was computed based on name of the dependency relation. A tree kernel then computed the similarity between two trees by recursively computing node similarity between two nodes as described in (Culotta and Sorensen, 2004). The only difference being, unlike our approach they have only word nodes in the tree. The kernel is hence a function $K(T1, T2)$ which computes similarity between two dependency trees $T1$ and $T2$. See (Culotta and Sorensen, 2004) for why K is a valid kernel function. However, we got poor results. In experiments involving within dataset evaluation, the tree kernel gave F1 scores of 77.0, 76.2 and 74.5 on NegCorp, BID and PH datasets respectively. We also tried constructing composite kernels, by adding kernel matrices of the tree kernel and the ABoW kernel or NF kernel, hoping that they captured complimentary similarities between assertions. Although performance of the composite kernel was better than the tree kernel itself, there was no significant gain in the performance as compared to those of the reported kernels.

7 Discussion

We observe that while the precision of all the classifiers is almost constant across all the set of experiments, it is the recall that changes the F1-score. This implies that the kernel fetches more cases than the baseline. The bag of words contributes towards the increase in recall and thus raises performance.

It is instructive to look at sentences that were misclassified by NegEx but correctly classified by the $ABoW_{gold}$ system. The NegEx rule-based system looks for specific phrases, before or after the target concept, as negation cues. The scope of the negation is determined using these cues and the presence of conjunctions. False positives stem from instances where the scope is incorrectly calculated. For example, in "No masses, neck revealed lymphadenopathy", the concept 'lymphadenopathy' is taken to be negated. The issue of negation scope being a shortcoming of NegEx has been acknowledged by its authors in Chapman et al. (2001). There were certain instances where the NegEx negation cues and the target concept overlapped. For example, in "A CT revealed a large amount of free air", the target concept 'free air' was wrongly identified by NegEx as negated. This is because 'free' is a post negation cue, to cover cases such as "The patient is now symptom free". Similarly, with 'significant increase in tumor burden' as the target concept, the sentence "A staging CT scan suggested no significant increase in tumor burden" was wrongly identified as an affirmation. Since the closest negation cue was 'no significant,' NegEx would identify only concepts after the phrase 'no significant' as negated. We also found interesting cases such as, the "Ext: cool, 1 + predal pulses, - varicosities, - edema." where the concept 'varicosities' is negated using the minus sign.

We studied cases where NegEx made the right decision but which were incorrectly classified by our system. For example, in the assertion "extrm - trace edema at ankles, no cyanosis, warm/dry", the kernel incorrectly classified "trace edema" as negated. In "a bone scan was also obtained to rule out an occult hip fracture which was negative", the concept "occult hip fracture" was incorrectly classified as affirmed. We found no evident pattern in these examples.

The tree kernel was constructed to automatically capture subtree patterns similar to those handcrafted by Sohn et al. (2012). Although, it resulted in a poor performance, there are a number of possibilities to improve the current model of the kernel. Clinical data often consists of multi-word expressions (e.g., "congestive heart failure"). However, the word nodes in our dependency tree kernel are unigrams. Aggregating these unigrams (e.g., identification using MetaMap, followed by use of underscores to replace whitespaces) to ensure they appear as a single node in the tree could give dependency parses that are more accurate. Similarity for nodes involving dependency tree relations; similarity in our kernel is a binary function examining identical names for dependency relations. This could be relaxed by clustering of dependency relations and computing similarity based on these clusters. We followed Culotta and Sorensen (2004) and used WordNet synonymy for similarity of word nodes. However, open-domain terminologies such as WordNet are known to be insufficient for tasks specific to the biomedical domain (Bodenreider and Burgun, 2001). This could be coupled with domain specific resources such as UMLS::Similarity (McInnes et al., 2009) for a better estimate of similarity. Finally, since learning structural patterns is a complex task achieved by the tree kernel; training with a larger amount of data could result in improvements.

8 Conclusion

We demonstrate the use of kernel methods for the task of negation detection in clinical text. Using a simple bag of words kernel with the NegEx output as an additional feature yields significantly improved results as compared to the NegEx rule-based system. This kernel generalizes well and shows promising results when trained and tested on different datasets. The kernel outperforms the rule-based system primarily due to an increase in recall. We also find that for instances where we do not have additional labeled training data, we are able to leverage the NegEx Corpus as a bootstrap to perform semi-supervised learning using kernel methods.

Acknowledgments

Research reported in this publication was supported by the National Library of Medicine of the National Institutes of Health under award number R01LM011116. The content is solely the responsibility of the authors and does not necessarily represent the official views of the National Institutes of Health.

References

Daniel Albright, Arrick Lanfranchi, Anwen Fredriksen, William F Styler, Colin Warner, Jena D Hwang, Jinho D Choi, Dmitriy Dligach, Rodney D Nielsen, James Martin, et al. 2013. Towards comprehensive syntactic and semantic annotations of the clinical narrative. *Journal of the American Medical Informatics Association*, 20(5):922–930.

Alan R Aronson. 2001. Effective mapping of biomedical text to the UMLS Metathesaurus: the MetaMap program. In *Proceedings of AMIA Annual Symposium.*, pages 17–21.

Olivier Bodenreider and Anita Burgun. 2001. Comparing terms, concepts and semantic classes in WordNet and the Unified Medical Language System. In *Proceedings of the NAACL 2001 Workshop: WordNet and other lexical resources: Applications, extensions and customizations.*, pages 77–82.

Olivier Bodenreider. 2004. The Unified Medical Language System (UMLS): integrating biomedical terminology. *Nucleic Acids Research*, 32(Database issue):D267–70.

Zou Bowei, Zhou Guodong, and Zhu Qiaoming. 2013. Tree Kernel-based Negation and Speculation Scope Detection with Structured Syntactic Parse Features. In *Proceedings of the 2013 Conference on Empirical Methods in Natural Language Processing*, pages 968–976.

Chih-Chung Chang and Chih-Jen Lin. 2011. LIBSVM: A library for support vector machines. *ACM Transactions on Intelligent Systems and Technology*, 2:27:1–27:27.

Wendy W Chapman, Will Bridewell, Paul Hanbury, Gregory F Cooper, and Bruce G Buchanan. 2001. A simple algorithm for identifying negated findings and diseases in discharge summaries. *Journal of Biomedical Informatics*, 34(5):301–10, October.

Wendy W Chapman, Dieter Hilert, Sumithra Velupillai, Maria Kvist, Maria Skeppstedt, Brian E Chapman, Michael Conway, Melissa Tharp, Danielle L Mowery, and Louise Deleger. 2013. Extending the NegEx lexicon for multiple languages. *Studies in health technology and informatics*, 192:677.

Aron Culotta and Jeffrey Sorensen. 2004. Dependency Tree Kernels for Relation Extraction. In *Proceedings of the 42Nd Annual Meeting on Association for Computational Linguistics*, ACL '04.

Marie-Catherine de Marneffe and Christopher D. Manning. 2008. The Stanford typed dependencies representation. In *Coling 2008: Proceedings of the workshop on Cross-Framework and Cross-Domain Parser Evaluation*, pages 1–8.

Marie-Catherine de Marneffe, Bill MacCartney, and Christopher D Manning. 2006. Generating Typed Dependency Parses from Phrase Structure Parses. In *Proceedings of LREC*, pages 449–454.

Christiane Fellbaum. 1998. *WordNet: An Electronic Lexical Database*. Bradford Books.

Henk Harkema, John N Dowling, Tyler Thornblade, and Wendy W Chapman. 2009. ConText: An algorithm for determining negation, experiencer, and temporal status from clinical reports. *Journal of Biomedical Informatics*, 42(5):839–851.

Thomas Hofmann, Bernhard Schölkopf, and Alexander J. Smola. 2008. Kernel methods in machine learning. *The Annals of Statistics*, 36(3):1171–1220, June.

Thorsten Joachims, Nello Cristianini, and John Shawe-Taylor. 2001. Composite Kernels for Hypertext Categorisation. In *Proceedings of the Eighteenth International Conference on Machine Learning*, pages 250–257. Morgan Kaufmann Publishers Inc.

Bridget T McInnes, Ted Pedersen, and Serguei V S Pakhomov. 2009. UMLS-Interface and UMLS-Similarity : Open Source Software for Measuring Paths and Semantic Similarity. In *Proceedings of the Annual AMIA Symposium.*, volume 2009, pages 431–5.

Sunghwan Sohn, Stephen Wu, and Christopher G Chute. 2012. Dependency Parser-based Negation Detection in Clinical Narratives. In *Proceedings of AMIA Summits on Translational Science.*

Brett R South, Shobha Phansalkar, Ashwin D Swaminathan, Sylvain Delisle, Trish Perl, and Matthew H Samore. 2006. Adaptation of the NegEx algorithm to Veterans Affairs electronic text notes for detection of influenza-like illness (ILI). In *Proceedings of the AMIA Annual Symposium*, pages 1118–1118.

György Szarvas, Veronika Vincze, Richárd Farkas, and János Csirik. 2008. The BioScope Corpus: Annotation for Negation, Uncertainty and Their Scope in Biomedical Texts. In *Proceedings of the Workshop on Current Trends in Biomedical Natural Language Processing*, BioNLP '08, pages 38–45.

Özlem Uzuner, Brett R South, Shuying Shen, and Scott L DuVall. 2011. 2010 i2b2/VA challenge on concepts, assertions, and relations in clinical text. *Journal of the American Medical Informatics Association : JAMIA*, 18(5):552–6.

Stephen Wu, Timothy Miller, James Masanz, Matt Coarr, Scott Halgrim, David Carrell, and Cheryl Clark. 2014. Negations Not Solved: Generalizability Versus Optimizability in Clinical Natural Language Processing. *PloS one*, 9(11):e112774.

Author Index